LEGIONARY

PHILIP MATYSZAK

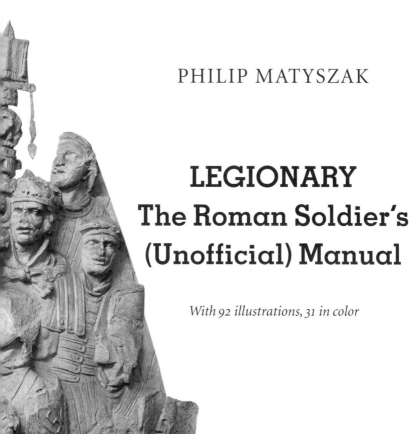

LEGIONARY
The Roman Soldier's
(Unofficial) Manual

With 92 illustrations, 31 in color

Thames & Hudson

To John Radford, Gunther Maser and
the others from 5 Group, Mrewa.

HALF-TITLE *Legionary's dagger and sheath. Daggers are
used for repairing tent cords, sorting out boot hobnails
and general legionary maintenance, and consequently
see much more use than a sword.*

TITLE PAGE *Trajan addresses troops after battle. A Roman
general tries to be near the front lines in a fight so that he
can personally comment afterwards on feats of heroism
(or shirking).*

First published in 2009 in hardcover in the United States of
America by Thames & Hudson Inc., 500 Fifth Avenue,
New York, New York 10110

thamesandhudsonusa.com

Library of Congress Catalog Card Number 2008908220

ISBN 978-0-500-25151-5

Printed and bound in China by SNP Leefung Printers Limited

Contents

I

Joining the Roman Army

*conscribe te militem in legionibus. pervagare orbem terrarum. inveni terras
externas. cognosce miros peregrinos. eviscera eos* *

✝ ✝ ✝

Rome needs you!

In this year, AD 100, one of the first years of the reign of the emperor Marcus
Ulpius Nerva Traianus (later known as Trajan), Rome's empire knows no
bounds. Our frontiers stretch to the deserts beyond distant Palmyra, and
across the bogs and mists of Britannia. Yet everywhere, Rome's security is at
risk. Scheming and subversive political elements foment rebellion within
the framework of the state, wild barbarians constantly probe the borders
for weakness, and the great and jealous power of Parthia threatens the
entire East. Against these multiple dangers stand two great towers of
defence – the wisdom and energy of our emperor, and the might of the
Roman army, which, ever faithful, protects and serves the Roman people.

Never has there ever been a better time to join the Roman army. Three
generations since the emperor Augustus put it on to a professional footing,
the military system has been fine-tuned to create the deadliest and most
sophisticated fighting force the world has ever seen. Everything is organized with Roman precision, from when a raw recruit signs on, until after he
has been pensioned off (or given a decent funeral). After 40 years of being
(militarily speaking) one of the most interesting places in the empire, the
defiant Britons have been largely subdued, and the glory days of campaigning in wet socks have come to an end. Attention is turning to the
troublesome kingdom of Dacia beyond the Danube, and after that, a final
reckoning with the Parthians awaits in the desert sands of Mesopotamia.

---

* Join the legions, see the world, travel to foreign parts, meet interesting and
exotic people, and disembowel them.

Marcus Ulpius Nerva Traianus, Imperator Optimus, ruler of Rome, master of the known world and your commander-in-chief. Here we see him in armour, with his general's red cloak draped over one arm. Born in Hispania Baetica (Spain) in AD 53, *Trajan has been emperor since* AD 98. *May his reign be long and glorious!*

The army of Rome possesses the world's most advanced and powerful weapons and equipment, making it second to none in terms of mobility, firepower and protection. A legionary might find his home in an army post anywhere in the empire, where he'll live and train to be at his best for when the army takes the field. For the right recruit, the army can provide direction, career opportunities and a steady income for the next 25 years. This manual will provide guidance for all of those years, from where and how to sign up, to the complexities of training, armour and drill. It will give you tips on surviving battle and life in camp, and finally guide you to a peaceful and prosperous retirement when your campaigning days are done.

Who can sign up?

Without the Roman army, there would be no Rome. Being a soldier is one of the city's proudest traditions. Most of Rome's emperors have been soldiers, and in the days of the Republic few politicians could face the voters and win office if they had not already faced Rome's enemies and won victories in the field. Romulus, Cincinnatus, Cato the Censor and Cicero all saw

The *Pax Romana* 'The Roman Peace'

The known world is entering into a period of unprecedented peace and prosperity which will be known to later generations as the *Pax Romana*. This 'peace' does not mean that the legions won't spend much of their time killing and getting killed by enemies outside the Roman frontiers, but within the borders of the empire there is an agreement between Rome and her subjects that the subjects will not rebel, and in return the legionaries will not burn down their cities and crucify the inhabitants. This policy works well, but requires emperors to have a degree of skill and competence, like those that Rome will be blessed with for most of the next century. Even the most benevolent emperors discreetly let potential trouble-makers know that they have a legion or two within pillaging distance.

A Roman recruiter, such as the man on the far right, might dream of a crush such as this (shown here on Trajan's column) of fresh, healthy recruits eager to sign up for a quarter-century of service with Roman legions. Any runaway slaves or wanted criminals in the queue can expect rejection and punishment.

----

military action. The men they commanded were Roman citizens, and citizens of good standing too, for the ranks of Rome's army were – and still are – closed against slaves, criminals and ne'er-do-wells.

✢ ✢ ✢

No youth born from parents such as those [ne'er-do-wells] could stain the sea with Carthaginian blood, nor throw down Pyrrhus, and mighty Antiochus, and the terrible Hannibal. No, it was the manly progeny of rustic soldiers, young men taught to turn the soil with Sabine spades, and to carry staves cut from the woods at the pleasure of a strict mother.

HORACE ODES 3.6

✢ ✢ ✢

So wrote the poet Horace, himself a country boy who served with the legions. Although Horace ingloriously ended his military career by dumping his shield and running for his life at the battle of Philippi in 42 BC, he has a point nevertheless. Roman recruits fall into three classes – those involuntarily conscripted (*lecti*), those who have been induced to volunteer in place of a conscript (*vicarii*) and those who really do want to join the army (*voluntarii*). A steady flow of Italian *voluntarii* of sound body and character turning up at the barrack gates is what every legionary recruiting officer dreams about.

For those who are thinking of spending the next two decades or so serving under the eagles of Rome, here is a quick checklist of what is required.

• Roman citizenship

In times of total desperation slaves and foreigners have been recruited into the legions. These are not such times. A *peregrinus* (non-citizen) wanting an army career should try the auxilia. A slave trying to get into the army will be sentenced to the mines, or even executed for his impertinence.

• Bachelor status

At this time Roman soldiers cannot be married. However, there is nothing to stop an unhappily married man from running away to join the legions. Roman marriage is a civil union rather than a religious sacrament, and joining the army serves as a unilateral declaration of divorce.

• A whole and healthy body

The Roman army likes to recruit from professions such as butchers and blacksmiths, or reapers who fancy a grimmer crop. Given the occupational hazards of such trades, the fingers on each applicant's hand are carefully counted. Lack of an index finger or a thumb is grounds for disqualification. There have been shameful cases in a *dilectus* (an emergency levy of conscripts) of people cutting fingers off to avoid military service. If deliberate mutilation is proven, the punishment is severe.

• A height of at least 5 ft 10 in.

Remember that the Roman foot is about one third of an inch shorter than later measures of the same name, and that exceptions may be made for particularly sturdy-looking individuals.

• A set of male genitalia

Females and eunuchs need not apply. It's a man's life in the legions. Some will be pleased to know that Trajan recently decreed that those who have lost but a single testicle can still serve.

• Good eyesight

> *Tryphon, son of Dionysius ... discharged by Gnaeus Vergilius Capito ... for having weak eyesight due to a cataract. Examined at Alexandria. Certificate dated in the 12th year of Tiberius Claudius Caesar Augustus Germanicus on 29 Pharmouthi.*
>
> DOCUMENT RELATING TO A RELEASE FROM MILITARY SERVICE ON 24 APRIL AD 52

• Good character

A past history of petty crime might be overlooked, but anyone who tries joining up to escape prosecution for a serious offence will be summarily ejected, as will those using the army as a means of sneaking back from exile. At this time, service in the legions is a privilege. How well or badly a military career starts off depends, as does so much else in Roman life, on personal contacts. Who recommends a recruit, and on what grounds, is crucial to that recruit's future career.

• The letter of recommendation

This letter is an essential first step, and anyone considering joining the army should make it his business to get as glowing a recommendation from as high-ranking a person as possible. Letters of recommendation are a common feature of Roman life and serve as references for a number of different circumstances. In recommending someone for the army, the writer is putting his own personal reputation on the line. Unsurprisingly, letters of recommendation from veteran soldiers tend to be very favourably received,

Trajan decides

Pliny [Governor of Bithynia in Asia Minor] to the emperor Trajan: *The very excellent young man Sempronius Caelianus, having discovered two slaves among the recruits, has sent them to me. But I deferred passing sentence till I had consulted you, the restorer and upholder of military discipline, concerning the punishment proper to be inflicted upon them.*

Trajan to Pliny: *Sempronius Caelianus has acted agreeably to my orders, in sending such persons to be tried before you as appear to deserve capital punishment. It is material, however, in the case in question, to enquire whether these slaves enlisted themselves voluntarily, or were chosen by the officers, or presented as substitutes for others [who were conscripted into military service]. If they were chosen, the officer is guilty; if they are substitutes, the blame rests with those who deputed them; but if, conscious of the legal inabilities of their station, they presented themselves voluntarily, the punishment must fall upon their own heads. That they are not yet entered into any legion makes no great difference in their case; for they ought to have given a true account of themselves immediately upon their being approved as fit for the service.*

PLINY THE YOUNGER *LETTERS TO TRAJAN*

especially if written by one who has served with the unit the prospective recruit wants to get into. Much also depends on how keen that unit is on taking in new recruits at the time an application is made. According to the satirist Juvenal, being at the right place at the right time counts for a lot.

Gallius, who can measure the benefits of a successful army career? I hope that I am under a lucky star when the gates of the camp welcome me as a terrified recruit. One moment of real good luck means more than a letter of recommendation from Venus to Mars, or one from his mother Juno ...

JUVENAL *SATIRES* 16 (1–6)

✣ ✣ ✣

If the legion does not need recruits, the volunteer might find himself in an auxiliary cohort, or even serving with the fleet. With a plentiful supply of recruits, those with the best recommendations get the best jobs. 'Hold this letter in front of your face and imagine that it is me, in person, talking to you', the writer of one such letter of recommendation urges a recruiting officer whom he evidently knows from his earlier military service.

What happens next?

Testing times

Having obtained the letter of recommendation – the first weapon a prospective recruit needs in a military career – the next step is to present oneself for an interview, the *probatio*. The *probatio* is exactly what the name implies. It is a test. This is conducted before the would-be legionary is sworn in and sent to his unit. The purpose of the *probatio* is to make sure that the man is who he claims to be, and also that he has a physique capable of withstanding the demands that will be made on it over the coming months and years. The letter of recommendation will be carefully scrutinized, and those conducting the interviews will make enquiries if they feel the need. Consequently, those entering under false pretences (such as Pliny's slaves mentioned previously) might initially pass the first hurdle, but find the slow nemesis of the Roman bureaucracy closing in on them later.

Swearing in

If the examining officer can find no fault with his prospective recruits, he will line them up for the Military Oath. Note the capital letters. Right until the moment he has sworn his Oath the potential recruit is a civilian, free to come to his senses and without further consequences bolt from the barracks like a frightened rabbit. After the Oath, he is a soldier of Caesar, and bolting is desertion with all the terrible punishment this entails (*see* Discipline p. 74). A moment's reflection is therefore a good idea at this point. What happens in the next few minutes will shape the next 25 years. Or the rest of your life – whichever is shorter.

'Step forward, recruit number one, and swear by various gods and unbreakable oaths that you will follow your commander wherever he may lead you. You will obey orders enthusiastically and without question. You relinquish the protection of Roman civil law and accept the power of your commanders to put you to death without trial for disobedience or desertion. You promise to serve under the standards for your allotted time of duty and not to leave before your commander discharges you. You will serve Rome faithfully, even at the cost of your life, and will respect the law with regard to civilians and your comrades in the camp. Congratulations. You are now a soldier of Rome. Next!'

Recruit number two may have to repeat the Oath again, but if there are a large number of bodies to be processed, after recruit number one has announced the full text, subsequent recruits can commit themselves by stepping forward and announcing *idem in me* – 'and the same goes for me'.

Checking and tagging

Once sworn in, the legionaries are carefully identified. That is, their names are recorded along with any moles, scars or distinctive marks by which they may be recognized as deserters masquerading as civilians, or picked out from among the piles of corpses on a battlefield.

✠ ✠ ✠

C. Minucius Italus to Celsianus: ... *Six recruits to be entered into the records. Names and identifying marks as follows ... M. Antonius Valens/age 22/scar on right forehead/ [etc. The list of recruits continues at some length.] Received via Priscus [rank of] singularis. Avidus Arrianus ... of the Third Cohort confirms that the original of this copy has been entered in the records of the cohort.*

OXYRHYNCHUS PAPYRUS 1022

✠ ✠ ✠

This record is item number two in the ever-growing documentation which will accompany the legionary through his career. The records are linked to the individual by the identifying marks described, and by the *signaculum* ('little identifier') which the legionary now receives in a little pouch to wear around his neck. The *signaculum* is a small lead tablet which serves the soldier in the same way that 'dog tags' will identify members of later armies.

In these times *signaculi* are also used to identify items of property or slaves, but it is an unwise civilian who draws the obvious inference between these two categories and soldiers while in the presence of the latter.

On the road

A small party of soldiers from the unit to which the new recruits are destined may be waiting to guide them to their new home, or the men may be instructed to make their own way to it. The legion's barracks may be a considerable distance from the recruiting station, so the recruits receive a *viaticum* – road money – to cover their expenses on the journey. If accompanied by an officer from their new unit the recruits will be expected to hand their money over to him, as the officer will have travelled the route before, knows the best places to stay, and can negotiate group rates for his party. Any leftover money is deposited into the recruit's account when he arrives at his destination.

Individuals or groups too small to merit an escort can choose to travel first class and arrive broke, or sleep rough and arrive with a nice little nest egg. This is a useful introduction to legionary life. As will be seen, there are many circumstances where it will be possible to choose between paying for relative comfort or gritting your teeth and working on your pension.

✣ ✣ ✣

Longinus Longus, standard-bearer of the First Lusitanian Cohort, to his centurion Tituleius Longinus: *I am in receipt of 423 denarii and 20 obols; the said sum being monies deposited by 23 recruits arrived at this centurio on Thoth 6 [3 September] in the 21st year of the noble Caesar, our lord Trajan.*

PAPYRUS FROM EGYPT, AD 117

✣ ✣ ✣

Arrival at one's unit is something a soldier never forgets. This is all the family that a legionary will have for the next 25 years.

II

The Prospective Recruit's Good Legion Guide

*milites exercitati facile intellegi possunt. abundant tamen tirones periculosi *

A quick history of the Roman army

Given that Rome has been around for some 700 years, it comes as a bit of a shock to realize that the state has had a proper professional army for less than a fifth of that time. Before then, to find a Roman soldier you had merely to stop any able-bodied Roman male on the street. It would be very probable that this man had spent the last few months under arms and returned to the city with his general – who would also be a Roman consul – at the end of the campaigning season.

500 BC

At this time, it was much easier to be a soldier because Rome's enemies were local. For instance, when Rome was fighting the Etruscans of Veii, some officers were able to pop home for supper. The campaigning season began in spring, when the army was enrolled, and ended in autumn when the army was disbanded so that the men could return home to help with the harvest. Every Roman soldier was a citizen – and vice versa. When the citizens assembled to vote for their leaders, they did so on the Field of Mars, formed up in their centuries as the Roman army. As a rough rule of thumb, a vote carried as much weight as the voter's military kit. The first to vote were the horsemen, the equestrians. Since horses are heavy, equestrian

---

* Professionals are predictable. The world is full of dangerous amateurs.

votes were extremely important. Next came the voters of the first class – those who could afford heavy armour, swords and shields. Obviously these were respectable citizens who should be listened to – not least because possession of such military kit meant that when these citizens were upset, the authorities could literally get the point about their complaint. Another consequence of this style of voting was that most major issues were generally decided by the equestrians and the first class before the rabble who brought slings and pointed sticks to battle had been given their say. (Which, in the opinion of the first class and equestrians, was no bad thing.)

300 BC

The original basic military unit of the army was the phalanx, a solid block of spearmen. However, this large, unmanoeuvrable unit was less than perfect for chasing highly mobile tribesmen around the mountains of Italy, so in the 4th century BC the army adopted the maniple. This was a 'handful' of men (from *manus*, the Latin for 'hand') or, more precisely, 120 men. The soldiers fought in three ranks of maniples.

The *hastati* were the front maniple, made up of raw soldiers inexperienced enough to be brave, and too young to value their lives. The men of this maniple were armed with swords and what is still today the legion's throwing weapon of preference – the heavy, short-range spear called the *pilum*.

The *principes*, the second maniple, did value their lives, and fought all the more grimly because they knew from experience that victory was their best guarantee of seeing their wives and families again. These soldiers were armed in the same manner as the *hastati*, though their armour might be better quality.

The *triarii* were the back-rank maniple, and contained veterans of the old school, fighting with the long spears of the phalanx, and who could be counted on to hold the line if all else failed. That is why, even now, the expression 'it's come to the *triarii*' means that matters have become desperate.

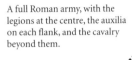

A full Roman army, with the legions at the centre, the auxilia on each flank, and the cavalry beyond them.

ABOVE *Bust believed to be of Gaius Marius. The reforms of Marius affected not only the Roman army but also had far reaching and not always positive effects on Roman history.*

RIGHT *Reconstruction of a manipular legion. The arrangement of the men into compact, semi-autonomous blocks gave the legion great flexibility which allowed the Romans to crush enemies such as the solid but unmanoeuvrable Macedonian phalanx.*

100 BC

The conservative Republican system was disrupted by the demagogic general Gaius Marius, who was in desperate need of soldiers. At the time Rome was fighting an expansionist war in Numidia and preparing for a defensive war against Germanic tribes in the north. Marius abolished the property regulation and got the state to provide military equipment. He also started the tradition of giving each legion an *aquila*, an eagle that represented Jupiter, as its principal symbol. Marius formed the legions into a basic battle formation, based around the cohort, and this is how they remain today.

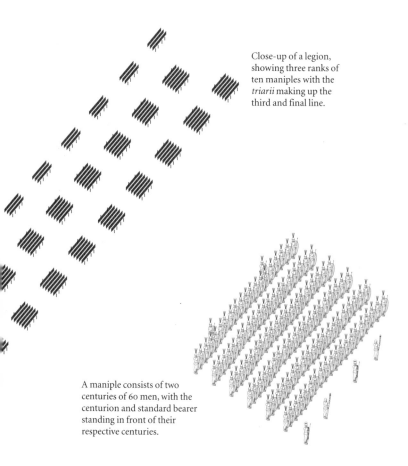

Close-up of a legion, showing three ranks of ten maniples with the *triarii* making up the third and final line.

A maniple consists of two centuries of 60 men, with the centurion and standard bearer standing in front of their respective centuries.

Although a good general, Marius often did not think through the consequences of his decisions, and his changes to the system solved short-term problems while storing up huge trouble for the future. Once the state started providing kit for the soldiers, the de-rustication of the army occurred, for the legionaries were now not only recruited from peasants but from the urban poor as well. As the city recruits had no harvests to

The cohort

Cohorts are of six centuries each, and since centuries have dropped in number from 100 to 80 men, this gives 480 men per cohort. Ten cohorts of 480 men makes a legion, or 6,000 soldiers. Those seeking a billet in the pay corps will have observed a discrepancy in the above figures. CDLXXX men multiplied by X cohorts does not come to MMMMMM soldiers. The extra bodies that do in fact make the number up to 6,000 are supplied by the first cohort, which is a double-strength unit of 800 men. In fact, 6,000 men is the very maximum including cooks and supernumeraries. In reality, the legions are always chronically under-strength, so 4,800 is probably nearer the actual number of men in the average legion.

come home to, many simply stayed under arms, re-enrolling year after year. This suited their generals, since Rome had started campaigning in distant places such as Greece and Spain. (To make sure that each year's army had reached the war zone by the start of the campaigning season, the beginning of the year was moved back to January, where it has remained ever since.) The problem came when, after about two decades of signing up every year, soldiers grew too old for service, and not unnaturally looked to the state for their pension.

✣ ✣ ✣

I am Spurius Ligustinus, of the Tribe Crustumina, and I come from Sabine stock. My father left me half an acre of land and the little hut in which I was born and brought up. I am still living there today … I have completed 22 years of service in the army, and I am now over 50 years old. But even if I had not completed my service, and if my age did not give me exemption, it would still be right for me to be discharged.

LIVY *HISTORY OF ROME* 42.34

✣ ✣ ✣

80 BC

The 'state' in this case meant the consuls who proposed the necessary legislation, and since the consuls were often beholden to – or actually were – the generals who had just completed a successful campaign, the soldiers started to look to their general to make arrangements for their post-military career. As political life in Italy grew more troubled, the generals became ever more important. With the threat of civil war looming, politicians rapidly discovered the wisdom of not annoying large numbers of freshly unemployed individuals who had considerable experience of heavy-duty combat. Getting their veteran troops peacefully retired onto a good patch of land became a priority for generals such as Sulla and Pompey, not least because by doing so the generals earned the gratitude of their veterans. And if the need arose, these veterans were generally willing to take up the sword again to repay the favour.

✛ ✛ ✛

He [Octavian] seized the consulship when he was 20. He quartered his legions menacingly close to the city [Rome], and sent messengers in the name of the army to demand the consulship for himself. When the Senate hesitated, the leader of the deputation, a centurion called Cornelius, presumptuously threw back his cloak to reveal the hilt of his sword. He informed the Senate that 'this will make him consul, if you will not'.

SUETONIUS *LIFE OF AUGUSTUS* 26

✛ ✛ ✛

31 BC

The political crisis came to a head in the 18 years between 49 and 31 BC, when the armies of Pompey fought those of Caesar, and then Octavian (later Augustus) fought Mark Antony. (For details of the great inter-Roman triumviral knock-out competitions known as the Civil Wars, the histories of Appian are recommended.) It is estimated that almost half a million men were called to arms in this 18-year period of civil strife. Even allowing for attrition of about 50 per cent through death, retirement or desertion along the way, this still left about 60 legions in service. Apart from those soldiers on duty elsewhere in the empire, 47 legions turned up

Silver denarius of Mark Antony issued just before the battle of Actium, and presciently featuring a trireme rigged for battle. Though more legions were present at Actium than at any other time in Roman history, many of the soldiers were mere spectators while the fate of the empire was decided at sea.

for the climax of the civil wars at the battle of Actium in 31 BC. Here Octavian fought Mark Antony and Cleopatra for mastery of the known world. When the smoke cleared, the last man standing was Octavian who, on adding Antony's men to his own forces, inherited one of the largest armies the world has ever seen.

The Augustan Settlement

Despite the many advantages of an ultra-large army, there was one insuperable flaw: The Roman state could not afford it. Even now, over 100 years later, the maintenance of the army is the largest drain on the treasury – in fact this expense, together with building operations such as roads (which are often done by the army anyway), is larger than all other government expenses put together. Octavian had to slim down the army quickly, and disband about 100,000 or so men in such a way that they did not resent their dismissal.

The solution was typical of Rome's shrewdest politician. Octavian was decisive, ruthless and effective. He simply took the land from well-off Italian communities and gave it to the ex-soldiers. There was considerable distress among the Italian peoples, but as the usurpers were ex-military, it would have been very unwise of them to protest too vigorously. Horace, the soldier-turned-poet mentioned above (p. 9), wrote his early poetry in bitter denunciation of the suffering that the settlement had caused in his home town. However, like many others, he was gradually converted into a pro-government stalwart by the benefits of the imperial peace.

It also helped that many of the soldiers now being stood down were conscripts eager to go home. Furthermore, the conquest of Egypt allowed

Octavian to give a cash bonus to those who did not want land, either in Italy or in the colonies which the imperial government planted abroad. Rome went from having 60 legions under arms to 28, at a short term cost of hundreds of millions of sesterces, but at a huge long-term saving.

After AD 6, the issue of settling soldiers after their retirement was put onto its present basis by the establishment of the *Aerarium Militare*, the Military Treasury. Augustus (as Octavian now styled himself) initiated the fund by paying 170 million sesterces of his own money into the pot, and thereafter insisted that the citizens of Rome keep the fund going through involuntary contributions, paid via a sales tax of one per cent on auctions, and five per cent on death duties (there is also a general two per cent tax for the Roman treasury – and, as we have seen, the army also gets a lot of this).

It would not be correct to say that Augustus took a semi-professional army of citizen-soldiers and reorganized it into a regular standing army, because the processes which created the Roman army of his day had been developing since before the time of Julius Caesar. However, Augustus certainly tidied things up and formalized arrangements, and the army he left after his death is recognizably the army of AD 100.

It was Augustus who fixed the term of service at 20 years (soon extended to 25), and who banned soldiers from getting married during this time. It is also thanks to Augustus' arrangements that a soldier being discharged can look forward to a pension that is the equivalent of about 14 years' pay.

Which legion?

Bear in mind that legions mostly recruit from their own catchment area, which tends to be the province they are stationed in. Therefore, a recruit looking for a particular billet needs to make sure that he enrols in the right place. So here's a quick guide to which legion goes where, with some comments on each legion's history. Life would be much simpler if the legions started with Legion I and worked their way up to Legion XXVIII, but history has put a number of kinks into this tidy arrangement.

First, even before the Augustan settlement, troubled times had meant that some legions had been in continuous existence long enough to develop their own identity and traditions. Some of these had been on Mark

Antony's side, and had surrendered only on the condition that the legion remained intact. This is why Legions X, XIII and XIV all have the name Gemina, meaning 'twin'. They are the result of amalgamations such as when an Augustan and Antonine legion of the same number were jammed together to form a single unit.

Anyone wanting to join Legions XVII, XVIII or XIX will need to take a dagger and kill himself in the gloomy depths of the Teutoburg forest in Germany, where these legions were wiped out in AD 9 in an ambush by the renegade Arminius. The numbers have never been used again, though the army was brought up to strength by Caligula's creation of two fresh legions called XV Primigenia and XXII Primigenia in AD 39. The name 'Primigenia' is probably a reference to Fortuna Primigenia, whom some believe to be Jupiter's first-born daughter. XV Primigenia surrendered to the enemy in AD 69 and was disbanded in disgrace along with several others. (Read the works of the historian Tacitus for the story of the revolts and wars of this period, which saw several legions wiped off the legionary list in disgrace.)

In about AD 66, Nero planned an expedition to conquer the area around the Caspian Sea, and added I Italica to the legion list – 'Italica' because the recruits were all Italians. Then with civil war brewing in AD 68, Nero needed a bit more military support and raised another legion by re-employing sailors from the fleet at Misenum (p. 45), which became I Adiutrix ('Supportive').

The army list of AD 100, after disasters and disbandments, recruiting and reconstituting, reads like this:

I Adiutrix

A good motto for this legion would be *ubique* – everywhere. The legion has served in Italy, Dalmatia and Moesia. Its soldiers can look forward to some hard fighting under the imperial standards in the coming Dacian and Parthian wars.

I Minerva

The name tells us that this legion was raised by the emperor Domitian, who adopted Minerva as his patron goddess. This is a new legion, less than 20 years old, and has been fighting in the same region as I Adiutrix, and has the same expectation of more fighting to come.

II Adiutrix

This is a legion, like I Adiutrix, originally made up of ex-sailors. This time the legion was formed by Vespasian to help in his struggle to become emperor. The legion plunged straight into battle in the Rhineland and then in Britain. After fighting in Wales and Scotland, it moved to the Dacian borders, and was soundly beaten by the warriors of that aggressive kingdom. Now stationed at Singidunum (Belgrade), it does much of its recruiting locally. An officer to watch from this legion is young Publius Aelius Hadrianus (Hadrian), who is tipped to have a stellar career.

II Augusta

Originally Spanish, this legion has been in Britain since AD 43. The legion is now making the best of the British climate at Isca Dumnonia (Exeter) and is expected to be there for some time. The legion's emblem is Capricorn, indicating it was reconstituted by Augustus who was born under that sign.

III Augusta

Changing the sign of Capricorn for Pegasus, the winged horse, transports you across the empire to the far sunnier climes of Africa. There is not a lot of fighting here, apart from occasional skirmishes with the desert horsemen of the Berbers, but the dates are good, both in terms of the fruit and assignations with local girls.

Both Capricorn and Pegasus, symbols of the II and III Augusta respectively, adorn this plaque of the Legio II Augusta. Many legions had an animal symbol, with the Gallic bull symbolizing those that served under Julius Caesar. The symbol of the Praetorian Guard was a scorpion.

III Cyrenaica

If you fancy the exotic land of the pyramids, look for a billet here, though be warned, once you have seen one sphinx you have seen them all. There are rumours that if the planned annexation of Arabia goes ahead the legion might see action instead of the usual fare of heat, flies and boredom, leavened with excitement when the Jews, Greeks and Egyptians of Alexandria have another go at destroying their city and each other.

III Gallicia

Despite its Gallic origins, this legion can be found in Syria. Those fighting under the standard of the bull can look eastward to wars with the Parthians, and westward in confident expectation of yet another rebellion in Judaea. Recommended for those who like their military service to be lively – and deadly.

IV Flavia Felix

Originally called Macedonica, this legion was renamed by Vespasian. As its bull emblem testifies, it was formed by Caesar. (Caesar's legions fought in Gaul, and the bull may be associated with a Gallic Bull-God.)

The legion was an early and loyal supporter of Octavian during the grim years before he became Augustus. During the civil war of AD 69 this legion struggled manfully to contain the restive German tribes, but later was distinctly lacklustre against fellow legionaries who defected to the enemy. Now with the name 'Felix', one assumes that the 'happy' or 'fortunate' part of its title refers to the legion's success in avoiding disbandment for lack of effort.

IV Scythica

A legion originally raised by Mark Antony from the peoples north of the Black Sea (hence the name). Switching its loyalty to Augustus after Actium, the legion adopted Augustus' symbol of Capricorn as its emblem. As with Legio XII Fulminata, its soldiers were defeated by both the Jews and the Parthians in the 60s, and the men are not considered prime combat material. The emperor Vespasian, if pushed, would bashfully admit to serving with this legion when young. Its soldiers have an excellent reputation as road-builders.

V Macedonica

A legion that knows how to pick its enemies. It has fought barbarians all over the northeast of the empire, with a brief excursion to Judaea for the Jewish War of AD 68. It is a firm favourite to be in the front line for the coming Dacian campaign, and has already been fighting off Dacian incursions together with II Adiutrix. Another legion with a bull emblem.

VI Ferrata (The Ironclads)

After helping to put Vespasian on the imperial throne in AD 70, this unit has gone east. It is currently on the banks of the Euphrates river, and may either join III Cyrenaica in Arabia, or be pulled back to hold down Judaea. Or both. In any case, another legion with interesting times ahead of it.

VI Victrix (The Victorious)

Currently at Vetera on the Rhine, where it took over from Flavia Felix (née Macedonica) and other legions which terminally embarrassed themselves by defecting to the enemy during the wars of AD 69–70. Mainly garrison duties, combined with taking on the Germans in minor raids, either as instigators or defenders. Every

now and then the general in charge of the Rhineland develops imperial ambitions, so a quick trip to Rome is an additional possibility.

VII Gemina

The most famous alumnus is the current emperor, Trajan, who was legionary legate in AD 89. This legion is 'Gemina' as it is an amalgam of the disgraced I Germanica, and VII Hispania. The Hispanic part has not moved far from home. Still stationed in Iberia, one of the empire's most peaceful provinces, recruits to this legion can look forward to the occasional patrol for bandits, garrison duty and pioneering the art of the siesta. This legion will stay in place so long that it will give its name to the town of Le(gi)on.

VII Claudia

This legion cut its teeth more than 150 years ago fighting under Julius Caesar in Gaul. In the event of civil war this is the legion to watch, as it has invariably supported the winner. Its legionaries fought for Caesar against Pompey in Spain and at Pharsalus, and for Caesar's successor Octavian at Philippi. The legion was in Dalmatia in AD 42 and suppressed a rebellion there, earning the name Pia Claudia Fidelis – 'faithful and true'. The legion backed Vespasian for emperor, and was instrumental in winning the battle of Cremona for him in AD 69. It is expected to be at the spearhead of the coming Dacian campaign.

VIII Augusta

This long-established legion is one of the army's best-kept secrets. Like VII Claudia it is a former Caesarian legion, and it is currently stationed at Argentoratum (Strasbourg). While some are appalled at the idea of those in charge of a pan-European empire doing very little apart from enjoying the local cuisine and wines, others feel it is a small price to pay for the prevailing peace and tranquillity.

IX Hispania

The legion's unofficial motto is 'don't mention Boudicca'. The British warrior queen gave this legion a severe mauling in her rebellion of AD 60–61, and some of the more sensitive veterans are still reputed to go all faint at the sight of woad. Currently the major enemy of the legion is rheumatism caused by the British damp. With the island at peace, the legion has

moved from Lindum (Lincoln) to Eboracum (York). In many years time this unit will transfer out of Britain with so little fuss that many will wonder what became of it, and it will go into legend as 'the lost legion'.

X Fretensis

After moving around the eastern Mediterranean, this legion is now stationed at Hierosolyma, the city the Romans established on the smoking ruins of Jerusalem after the rebellion of AD 66–68. A good posting for insensitive types who do not mind the locals spitting on their shadow as they walk by. Titus, the general at the time, ended up with a Jewish princess as a girlfriend. Local garrison troops should not expect such luck, but at least you have the emperor's sympathy. Trajan's father commanded a legion here during the revolt, and so Trajan knows what the soldiers have to deal with.

X Gemina

Originally one of Caesar's legions (and one which invaded Britain with him in AD 55), this legion was re-formed for the civil wars by the triumvir Lepidus, but quickly transferred its support to Augustus.

Desperate times at Castra Vetera

Many legions would like to forget their inglorious role in the civil wars and revolts of AD 69–70, and none more so than those in the debacle at Castra Vetera (Xanten). The Batavians, a tribe living along the Rhine, rose in rebellion led by one of their commanders, a Roman citizen called Julius Civilis. (The Romans had recently executed his brother so Civilis had a right to be bitter.) The legions V Alaudae, XVI Gallica and XV Primigenia failed to suppress the revolt. Eventually IV Macedonica and XXII Primigenia were drawn in along with I Germanica.

V Alaudae and XV Primigenia were besieged in the legionary camp of Castra Vetera, and defected to Civilis. I Germanica and XVI Gallica came marching to the rescue, but ended up surrendering as well. It took a large proportion of what remained of the Roman army to sort out the subsequent mess. In the eventual settlement XV Primigenia was disbanded outright. Threatened with the same fate, V Alaudae survived, only to be taken apart later by the Dacians. XVI Gallica and IIII Macedonica were renamed as XVI Flavia Firma, and IV Flavia Felix and I Germanica was merged with Legio VII to become as VII Gemina.

After a relaxing spell in Spain, it has recently found itself in the Rhineland. A good posting for anyone interested in carpentry, as the legion is currently battling with saw and mattock to build forts and dikes along the frontier.

XI

Officially another Pia Claudia Fidelis, this is pretty much an anonymous workhorse of a legion. Stationed in Vindonissa (in Switzerland), it went west to help put Vespasian on the throne, and to sort out the mess caused by the defection to the enemy of Macedonica, XV Primigenia et al. in AD 70. Currently in the Balkans, Legion XI will probably take over garrison duty in Pannonia after the fighting legions move into Dacia.

XII Fulminata (The Thunderbolts)

A legion that lives well below the expectations suggested by its thunderbolt symbol. Its members failed to conquer Armenia in AD 62, and surrendered to the Parthians, before then going on to lose their eagle to Jewish rebels in AD 66. After spending a while in eastern Cappadocia (Turkey) in the hope that nothing dangerous would come near it, this legion has transferred east to the Euphrates.

XIII Gemina

Yet another of the Gemini clan, this time with the symbol of a lion. Its proudest moment was in crossing the Rubicon with Caesar to kick off the civil wars of 49 BC. Reformed by Augustus, this legion has been stationed in the Danube region almost ever since. It did briefly head for Italy, fighting alongside VII Claudia to help make Vespasian emperor in AD 69, but basically its members are Dacian fighters *par excellence.*

XIV Gemina

Suppression of rebellions a speciality. This legion took part in the invasion of Britain in AD 43. It became the emperor Nero's

- - - - - - - - - -

Gnaeus Musius who joined the legions at the age of 17 and died aged 32 after serving 15 years. He was the standard bearer of Legio XIV Gemina and proudly displays the insignia on his shield, his standard and the torques he was awarded. The memorial was erected by his brother, a centurion.

favourite by defeating Boudicca in AD 61, and received the title 'Martia Victrix' as a reward. Moving to Germany, it helped to restore order after the troubles of AD 70. The only time it chose the wrong side was in supporting the imperial ambitions of the rebel governor, Saturninus, in AD 89. It is currently transferring to Vindobona (Vienna), though some detachments are preparing to join the Dacian campaign.

XV Apollinaris

Named after Apollo, the patron god of its founder Augustus, Apollinaris is from the region of Vindobona that XIV Gemina is moving into. XV Apollinaris saw some hard fighting in the Jewish rebellion, and is now preparing to put the Parthians to the test.

XVI Flavia Firma

Another of the victims of the debacle of AD 70, it is to be hoped that 'Firm for the Flavians' does better than it did in its previous incarnation as XVI Gallicia, which meekly surrendered to the enemy. The reconstituted legion was then stationed in Syria – and suspects rightly that this exile was intended as punishment of its mainly Gallic troops by Vespasian. The legion will

have a chance to redeem itself in the coming Dacian campaign.

This gap is in memory of those legions destroyed in the Teutoburg forest in AD 9 and never reconstituted. *Resquiescant in pace.*

XX Valeria Victrix

'Valour Victorious' is the motto of this legion, which is now resting on its laurels after a successful campaign against the Caledonians. Making up a third of the British legions (Britain has more garrisons for its size than anywhere else in the

The boar of Legio XX. The boar was a Celtic battle symbol, but the shape of the baked clay on which it is displayed shows that this was a tile antefix from the legion pottery, designed to stop the wind from getting under the curved roof tiles of barrack buildings.

empire, including Judaea, which is saying something), Valeria Victrix has a good reputation and no fighting in prospect. It is likely to be in Britain for a while.

XXI Rapax

The 'predators' successfully supported Vespasian in AD 69, and then backed the wrong horse in AD 89 when they were spectacularly unsuccessful in a rebellious attempt to make their provincial governor Saturninus emperor of Rome. They are currently garrisoning the lower Danube, and can expect to be there for a decade or two more until they have lived down their embarrassment.

XXII Deiotariana

Has the distinction of being non-Roman in origin, being formed from two legions raised by the Galatian king Deiotarus and constituted along Roman lines. This was so successful an imitation of a Roman force that Augustus incorporated it into the real thing. Like VII Gemina/Hispania, Deiotariana has not moved far from its roots, and is currently with III Cyrenaica brushing up its anti-riot skills in Alexandria.

XXII Primigenia

A legion which consistently picked the wrong side in the civil wars of AD 69, and then returned, somewhat chastened, to the business of garrisoning the Rhine frontier. This is a legion of hardened German fighters who have been at it for the last three generations. They picked up the title Pia Fidelis, 'loyal and faithful', for helping the emperor Domitian defeat the usurper Saturninus. A good choice for those who like to do one thing (kill Germans), but do it well.

✣ III ✣

Alternative Military Careers

conare levissimus videri, hostes enim fortasse instrumentis indigeant *

✣ ✣ ✣

There is more to the Roman army than just the legions – indeed, for some the legions might not even be the best choice. Below are some alternatives which an aspiring recruit might consider, though note that these positions are not all open to everyone. In whatever unit a soldier finds himself, he is nevertheless part of an integrated fighting force, supported by the complementary strengths of its different units.

The cavalry

Quick summary

Pros:

1 Soldiering on horseback is prestigious. The Roman aristocracy used to do it.
2 Why walk if you can ride?
3 Much of any battle is spent in reserve.
4 The cavalry is open to citizens and non-citizens alike.
5 If things get really tough on campaign, a horse provides several weeks worth of meat rations.

Cons:

1 There is a lot of kit to clean and maintain.
2 There is also a horse to groom and muck out.
3 The Parthian cavalry is generally superior to the Roman.
4 So is the Sarmatian cavalry.
5 And the Gallic, and the German, and the Numidian ...

---

* Try to appear unimportant – the enemy might be low on ammunition.

In earliest times [the Romans] fought without armour ... which put them at severe risk in close combat ... their spears were so light and bendy that they bounced with the horse's motion and were both impossible to throw properly and sometimes even broke before they were used in combat ... the shields were of ox-hide, too soft to be useful in attack, and once rain had rotted the skin, it peeled off, making the shield not just useless but a positive encumbrance.

POLYBIUS *HISTORIES* 6.25

Horses for courses

Things have changed since the days of the early Roman Republic that Polybius writes about, not least because the Romans have since got around the inferiority of their native cavalry by contracting out the work to nations with superior abilities on horseback. Because of the different techniques and requirements of cavalry in various parts of the empire, there is greater variety in the cavalry arm of the service than in any other part of Rome's armies.

For an example of this consider the cavalry of the eastern provinces, which have to deal with two totally different types of enemy on horseback. First, there are the lightly armoured bowmen who can shoot backwards over the rumps of their horses. This is the famous 'Parthian shot' which makes these riders as deadly when running away as when they are attacking. Secondly, the same region produces the fearsome *cataphracti*, cavalry with horses almost as heavily armoured as their riders. In each case the Roman cavalry have to adapt to the challenge of fighting very different enemies. For example, in the deserts of Numidia, the Romans have found that slingshots are a useful weapon against their mobile and ferocious Berber foes.

To my brother Heraclides, greetings. I've already written to you about young Pausanias wanting to serve in the legions. Well now he has decided he wants the cavalry ... I went down to Alexandria and tried various ways and means, and finally got him into a cavalry unit at Coptos ...

OXYRHYNCHUS PAPYRUS 1666

A mail-armoured cavalryman. Note the arm in position to hold a lance for an underarm thrust. Note also that the sword is longer than the legionary version, and the neck-guard of the helmet is shorter, though since this is the cavalry, generous provision has been made for affixing display plumes. Practicality and national taste have also resulted in this rider preferring trousers to tunic.

Roman horsemen are likely to find themselves in the legionary cavalry, units that are very closely integrated with the legions from which most of their members are drawn. Consider, for example, Tiberius Claudius Maximus, a Roman citizen from Philippi in Macedonia who enrolled in the army about 15 years ago. Naturally, he chose the legion in which his father had been a soldier before him – in this case VII Claudia – and because of his family connections he became a legionary cavalryman. He later transferred to the second Pannonian cavalry where he is today – a junior officer with a very respectable salary of 700 denarii a year. He was at one point on the staff of the legion commander – citizen cavalrymen are very useful couriers – but is now in charge of a troop of *exploratores*. These cavalrymen have the task of ranging out far ahead of the army, performing special missions or seeking intelligence of enemy movements. It is an interesting life, full of unexpected adventure, but it needs agility and fitness even greater than that expected of an average legionary.

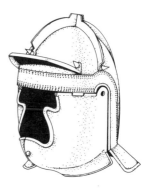

Cavalry helmet. Roman horsemen have helmets for battle, helmets for display and helmets for particular types of foe. The owner of this particular helmet evidently expects to be hit over the head a lot (note the cross brace) and has extensive protection from slashing weapons. However, hearing is important to a cavalryman in battle, so earholes enable both this and some ventilation.

Kit and equipment

There is an infantry joke that a cavalryman will never lack work when he reverts to civilian status. He can always find a job grooming horses. It is certainly true that a horseman has a busy life, both while in action and while preparing for it. Cavalry equipment is mostly modelled on that of the Celts who have provided the backbone of the cavalry over the past century. Expect to take and maintain the following on campaign:

Body armour This is usually chain mail, either Celtic style or as worn by the regular auxiliaries, but some units prefer scale armour.

Helmet This is significantly different from the infantry version, and needs a lot of getting used to. It is designed to give all-round protection in mounted melees, where attacks from behind happen more often than they do to legionaries. Cavalry helmets also lack the distinctive protruding protection that an infantry helmet has at the back, since falling on this protrusion from the height of a horse considerably increases the likelihood of a broken neck.

Shield A lot depends on where the unit is and what it is doing, but the standard shield is a flat oval, similar to those used by the auxiliaries. It takes a lot of practice to learn to use shield, sword, spear and javelin while sitting on a fast-moving horse. Practice at falling off the horse without severely injuring oneself occurs incidentally during the course of normal training.

Sword This is called the *spatha*. It is longer than the legionary *gladius* (p. 62) and often tucked under the saddle blanket when action is not anticipated.

Javelin A Roman horseman is a veritable missile platform. A charging cavalryman is expected to have discharged well over a dozen javelins or large darts at his opponents before the hand-to-hand fighting begins.

Saddle A particularly important item for a cavalryman is the distinctive Roman four-horned saddle. This, like the cavalry sword, was derived from the Celts, and is the only thing keeping the rider securely on his horse – the idea of dangly metal footrests (later known as stirrups) has not yet occurred to anyone. However, do not expect this lack of footrests to excuse a cavalryman from taking on infantry in combat – the saddle is deep and firm enough to allow tucking the spear underarm for a solid thrust without the rider being propelled backward over the horse's haunches on impact.

Harness and tack There is rather a lot of this, as the Romans like their cavalry to look impressive. So there are various medallions and other bits of metal to shine, as well as leather and buckles to keep in good condition.

Then there is the cavalryman's personal kit, and that's besides the care and maintenance of the horse itself.

On the battlefield, most cavalry fight in *alae*, literally 'wings', since they are generally stationed on the flanks of the infantry. As horses tire more quickly than humans, a cavalryman can expect to spend a good part of any

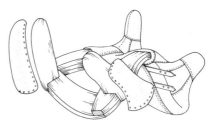

Four-horned saddle, showing the skeleton and attachment. A Roman rider relies on the vice-like grip of his thighs to stay in the saddle. The horns on the sides also help, though a rider getting on his horse in a hurry needs to take care not to become more securely mounted than he intended.

battle waiting in reserve – few commanders like to have more than half of their cavalry committed at once. Another major use of the cavalry in battle is when an enemy unit has been defeated and the cavalry are unleashed to ride down the broken and fleeing enemy. Being more sensible than humans, cavalry horses will not usually charge directly into formed-up units of enemy infantry or horsemen. Therefore when cavalry versus cavalry actions do occur, these are consensual affairs in which both sides open their ranks as they charge, so that the impact with the opposition occurs at speed and is both exhilarating and deadly. Otherwise the two sides may walk their horses at each other in close formation before beginning a full-scale hacking contest.

In barracks, part of the job of the cavalry is to give the locals a show. Trotting in shiny armour, behind an impassive face-mask, the cavalryman makes a proud sight. Tubular dragon banners fly over the troop (a cavalry troop is called a *turma*), and the horses have jingling metal plates decorating their harness. At moments like this the Roman cavalryman might feel it was worth the long hours of careful polishing, oiling and grooming, exercise and drill which it took to get the overall effect together.

It is difficult for cavalry attached to an [infantry] cohort to win approval by themselves, or even avoid initial adverse comment when they perform immediately after auxiliary cavalry have thrown more javelins and covered a larger amount of ground in their manoeuvres.

HADRIAN TO THE CAVALRY UNIT OF THE 6TH COMMAGENE COHORT,
IN AN INSCRIPTION AT LAMBAESIS
INSCRIPTIONES LATINAE SELECTAE, 2487

The auxilia

Quick summary

Pros:

1 Units tend to stay local.
2 Units are less regimented than the legions.
3 There are opportunities to use any specialist skills you may have.
4 One can serve with many fellow nationals.
5 There is an offer of Roman citizenship on discharge.

Cons:

1 The pay is lower than that of the legionaries.
2 The pension plan is inferior to that of the legionaries.
3 Relocation is often semi-permanent.
4 Auxilia are more involved in low-intensity warfare.
5 Units are regarded as more expendable than legionaries.

Background briefing

Those who can't ride a horse, are not Roman citizens, and who don't have influential connections will probably end up in the auxilia – or properly speaking, the other auxilia, since most cavalry are also auxiliaries. However, the term is generally used to refer to those lighter-armed, non-citizen infantry who do the riskier work for about 80 per cent of the pay. Service is for 25 years, but as you become a citizen on discharge, it is technically possible to join the auxilia at age 16, and then enrol in the legions at age 41, but many find that being in the army for over two decades cures their desire for a military career.

One thing to remember is that there have been auxilia almost as long as there has been a Roman army, though these were sometimes called 'allies', or at other times were even mercenaries. (In the 2nd century BC the Senate complained to Crete that it was supplying the archery for both Rome and their opponents – sometimes on the same battlefield.) There have also been as many, or even more, soldiers serving in the auxilia than in the legions, and this is still the case. As with most things military, the auxilia was put on a regular footing by Augustus, though the system is nowhere near as regimented as the legions.

Auxiliary service

An auxiliary can expect to serve in a cohort of about 480 men, most of whom will be his fellow nationals. Some auxiliaries may serve a long way from the place where they were recruited (even Caesar included Spanish slingers and cavalry, German horsemen and Cretan bowmen among his forces in Gaul), but once they arrive somewhere, the auxilia tend to remain there for a while. Losses are made up locally and the nationality of the cohort will change over time. So the cohort I Augusta, originally from Lusitania in Hispania, is now in Egypt and has acquired a contingent of 20 camel cavalrymen (*dromedarii*) who certainly didn't learn their skills in the Pyrenees.

As the presence of camel cavalry indicates, life in the auxilia has a certain informality that would not be found in the legions. For a start, because they operate in cohorts, the auxilia lack the administrative structure of the legion. This makes them very suitable for service in *vexillationes* – small units assembled ad hoc for special purposes. Auxilia might, for example, spend as much time traipsing behind tax collectors in a minor province as they do confronting barbarian hordes. There is also greater flexibility in the matter of arms and armour. After all, why take in Syrians (famed for their prowess with the bow) and equip them with a spear and a short sword? Especially as infantry bowmen are a sovereign cure for the light horse archers who plague the legions campaigning in the East.

This flexibility may be the reason why some Roman citizens actually choose to serve in the auxilia rather than the legions. This is particularly true of citizens who have grown up in a province and fancy a cavalry career with their fellow provincials. However, others join the auxilia as *pedites* (as the infantry are known) even though their citizenship entitles them to become legionaries. Their decision may be influenced by the fact that the auxilia are much more likely to stay close to home. The legions move around as the grand strategy of the empire requires. On the whole, the auxilia wave them a fond goodbye, and attach themselves to the new legion when one turns up. The result is that many non-citizen auxiliaries are in place long enough to acquire wives and raise families who are naturalized with them as Roman citizens on discharge. If these children follow daddy's

Which cohort?

The somewhat idiosyncratic system for naming legions is a paragon of military order compared to the auxilia. Auxiliary cohorts are named after their current location, or where they came from, or their tribal affiliation, or their favourite weapons, or the emperor when the unit was raised, or their commanding officer, or any combination of the above – usually with an apparently random number stuck on the front. However, this abundance of nominal options does not prevent different cohorts having the same name. There are at least two cohorts called I Alpinorum currently running around lower Pannonia, and if brevity does not equal clarity in their case, the same cannot be said for the sonorously named II Augusta Nervia Pacensis Brittonum who fight alongside them.

footsteps into the army – as many do – they give *castris* (the camp) as their place of origin, and have the choice of serving in their father's old auxiliary unit or the legions.

There are a number of reasons for keeping auxiliary cohorts in the same place:
• Local troops prefer to serve locally.
• In low-intensity warfare of ambushes, raids and skirmishes, local intelligence is vital.
• Low-intensity warfare requires soldiers who understand and respect local tradition.
• Local auxiliaries have spent centuries evolving weapons and fighting techniques best adapted to the terrain (for example there is little call for Numidian horsemen in the forests of Germany, while Batavian infantry from Lower Germania – excellent swimmers who specialize in crossing flooded rivers – might feel unemployed in the African desert which the Numidians call home).

The exception to generally keeping auxiliaries local is specialist troops, who are welcome anywhere. Sarmatian cavalrymen and Syrian archers, for example, really can expect to join the army and see the world. Their countrymen are scattered across the empire from the bogs of Britain to the bazaars of Alexandria.

Tiberius Julius Abdes Pantera from Sidon is buried here. He lived 62 years and was for 40 years a soldier in the cohort of archers.

TOMBSTONE AT BINGEIUM GERMANIA DESSAU
INSCRIPTIONES LATINAE SELECTAE, 2571

✛ ✛ ✛

Auxiliaries and legionaries

With regard to the legions, the role of the auxilia is exactly what their name means in Latin – help and support.

As the legions move toward battle the auxilia will be:
• scouting the terrain ahead for ambushes.
• briefing the general on the probable composition and tactics of the enemy.
• pointing the army in the direction of suitable food supplies and camp sites.

If it comes to a major battle, then the auxilia do not simply stand aside and let the legions take charge of proceedings. As the armies clash, the auxilia will be doing any, or all, of the following:
• the preliminary skirmishing.
• keeping hostile cavalry off the flanks of the legions.
• holding hilly or broken ground where the legionaries have trouble keeping formation.
• propelling spears, arrows or slingshots at the enemy according to speciality.
• fighting in the thick of it (though somewhat more lightly armed than the legionaries, the auxilia are probably better armed, trained and equipped than the enemy's main strike force, and may be expected to go head-to-head against it).

And of course, when the legion has gone back to camp, it is the auxilia who will form the local garrisons, patrol the land and set about the day-to-day business of maintaining the *Pax Romana* on the ground.

Vespasian marched out of Ptolemais, having ... ordered the lightly armed auxiliaries to march first with the archers, so that they might prevent any sudden attacks from the enemy, and search out any woods that looked suspiciously as though they might contain ambuscades.

JOSEPHUS *THE JEWISH WAR* 6.2

The navy

Quick summary

Pros

1 The navy provides a possible route out of slavery.
2 There are many opportunities for travel to exotic locations.
3 One can mess about in boats and use catapults and other exciting weapons.
4 There is an offer of citizenship on discharge.
5 If the fleet is based at Misenum one gets to operate the huge sunshade over the Amphitheatrum Flavium (the Colosseum).

Cons

1 The navy is despised by the other armed forces.
2 Sailors are sometimes required to work as impromptu land troops.
3 Rowing a *trireme* is hard work.
4 The minimum contract is longer even than that for auxiliary service.
5 Ships are liable to sink unexpectedly and catastrophically.

Background briefing

Legionaries are somewhat scornful of the navy, and are eager to tell of its role in the first Punic war, when it transported almost a quarter of a million men straight to the bottom of the sea without any help from the enemy. More recently, during the reign of the emperor Tiberius, a Roman campaign against the Marsi ended when a storm wiped out the fleet and a substantial proportion of the army. Bits of ship and drowned legionaries were still washing up on the German coast weeks afterwards.

A hailstorm blew up, and the waves rolled about in the wind blasting from all directions. The black mass of clouds blocked the view and made steering difficult. The soldiers were unused to emergencies on the high seas and discomforted the sailors by their terror. Their clumsy efforts to help cancelled out the work of the skilled crews.

TACITUS *ANNALS* 2.23

✠ ✠ ✠

Nevertheless, despite being the Cinderella of the Roman military, and having occasional problems staying afloat, the navy is worth consideration. It is hard to deny that there is a certain quirky appeal in the force which holds the all-time record for naval battles fought in land-locked Switzerland (just one, during the Augustan era, when the navy took on the Raetian and Vindelician fleets at the battle of Lake Constance).

The last major battle that the navy fought at sea was also the battle which ended Rome's century of civil wars and made Augustus emperor of Rome. This was the battle of Actium, in Greece in 31 BC, when the Roman and Egyptian navies met in a decisive clash. There are now no major enemy

OPPOSITE *The fleet comes in. Ships from the Roman navy make a landing at a Danubian river port. Although the ships and sailors are not in correct proportion, the sculptor had vividly shown the crowded conditions in which the oarsmen work, and the bulging biceps that one acquires in the course of the job.*

fleets, and those who dread ending up in a watery grave as an involuntary sacrifice to Neptune will be relieved to know that the modern navy does all its serious campaigning on rivers, with dry land reassuringly close to hand on each side.

✛ ✛ ✛

He could not even stand up to review the fleet when the ships were drawn up at battle stations. He was flat on his back staring at the sky, and did not even get to his feet to show his men he was alive until Marcus Agrippa had routed the enemy for him.

THE FUTURE AUGUSTUS IN BATTLE AT SEA (WITH SEASICKNESS?)
IN SUETONIUS *LIFE OF AUGUSTUS* 16

✛ ✛ ✛

The main arms of the navy are:

The *Classis Misenensis*, and the *Classis Ravennantis*. (A Roman fleet is called a *classis*, so *triremes* and *quinqueremes* are classic Roman warships in every sense.) The Misenum fleet is called after the cape of that name, and cruises the waters of the bay of Naples, though the entire western Mediterranean comes under its purview. The mandate of both this fleet

and that on the other side of the Italian peninsula at Ravenna is to escort the Alexandrian grain fleet and to suppress piracy. The latter especially concerns the Classis Ravennantis, as the peoples of Dalmatia and Liburnia on the eastern Adriatic coast have long regarded piracy as both a hobby and a lifestyle, and have no intention of letting the *Pax Romana* get in their way.

The **Classis Pannonica** and the **Classis Moesica**. Those looking for more organized opposition will find it by joining either the former, based near Aquincum (Budapest to later generations), or the latter, which operates further down the Danube and makes occasional forays into the Black Sea. Both fleets are expected to be busy in the coming campaign against the Dacians.

The **Classis Germanica.** On the other side of Europe, the Rhine fleet, based at Colonia Agrippinensis (Cologne), has to cope with those pesky aquatically skilled Batavians who are not on the Roman side. This fleet's duties also take it into the North Sea, where many sailors discover that evolution in the tideless Mediterranean does not perfectly equip triremes for the extremes of Atlantic wind and wave.

The **Classis Alexandria.** Perhaps the most romantic posting in the whole Roman military. This fleet not only has the job of cruising the palm-fringed banks of the Nile, but also makes excursions to the eastern Mediterranean. This was the last Roman naval force to see serious action, fighting against an impromptu fleet raised by nautically minded Jewish rebels in the war of AD 68–70. Another sideline of the Alexandrian fleet is escorting traders across the Persian Gulf to India, and there are rumours that crews of the Alexandria fleet will also find themselves operating along the river Euphrates, and sailing up to Babylon.

The only criterion for joining the navy is that you should be physically fit and have nothing else to do for the next 26 years or so. A mechanical aptitude is also useful, as apart from the technicalities of oars and rigging, Roman warships sport a fascinating array of incendiary devices and catapults (including one which fires grappling hooks). Salt spray and shipboard shaking means these devices all require constant maintenance.

While sailors are free men, some will have been freed especially for their new career. On completing their term of duty, sailors receive the same offer of citizenship as auxiliaries.

The Praetorians
Quick summary

Pros:

1 The Praetorians are stationed in Rome.
2 Their contracts are shorter than other military.
3 There is excellent pay and leave conditions.
4 They receive a large bonus when a new emperor takes over.
5 There are good prospects of moving to higher things on retirement.

Cons:

1 Occasionally the Praetorians do some actual soldiering if the emperor goes on campaign.
2 That's about it, actually.

Do the Praetorian cohorts, which have just got their two denarii per man, and who after 16 years are restored to their homes, encounter more perils? We do not disparage the guards of the capital; still, here amid barbarous tribes we have to face the enemy from our tents.

MUTINOUS SOLDIER AD 14, TACITUS *ANNALS* 1.1

Background briefing

The Praetorians are every legionary's dream posting. Praetorians are stationed in Rome itself, and only leave the capital when their imperial master goes on campaign. The pay is better, and the term of service is shorter. Yet this is only the half of it. Because the Praetorians are the largest military

An unfortunate misunderstanding

It is true that the current relations between the emperor Trajan and the Praetorians are not as good as they might be. The Praetorians violently objected to the man that Nerva (Trajan's predecessor) had chosen as his heir. Tense discussions between palace and Praetorians followed, which included the violent deaths of several imperial functionaries, and threats against the emperor himself. These resulted in Nerva publicly abandoning his proposed successor and announcing that the Praetorians' favourite, Trajan, would succeed him as emperor.

Those who had put him on the throne might have expected a little gratitude from the new emperor, but in fact one of Trajan's first acts was to arrest and execute those Praetorians who had terrorized his predecessor. Since Trajan has the whole-hearted backing of the Rhine legions, and the Praetorians would not fare well against these more numerous and combat hardened-troops, the emperor's guard have simply had to make the best of the current situation.

force in the capital, their loyal support is essential to an emperor's well-being. It is a wise emperor who ensures that the Praetorians are suitably rewarded for the care that they take of his imperial person. Gaius Caligula met his end when leaders of the Praetorian Guard decided against his suitability as emperor, and after Caligula's assassination it was the Praetorian Guard that forced the Senate to recognize Claudius as emperor. More recently the emperor Domitian (assassinated in AD 96) yet again increased Praetorian pay and privileges – though Praetorian arrogance does not make them universally popular in the capital.

OPPOSITE *Nice work if you can get it. Officers and troops of the Praetorian Guard looking appropriately smug about getting the best posting, pay and conditions in the entire Roman army.*

✛ ✛ ✛

The soldiers can more easily intimidate a witness into lying against a
civilian than an honest witness can impugn these golden boys in armour,
and that's before I mention the other perks of their job.

JUVENAL *SATIRES* 16 (32–35)

✛ ✛ ✛

Terms of service

The Praetorians take their name from the *praetorium*, the campaign tent of
the general in an army camp. The soldiers with the job of guarding the tent,
the 'Praetorians', gradually came to be known as the general's elite troops.
Their special status was formalized by Augustus (naturally), and the

Praetorian Guard took more or less its present form under Augustus' successor Tiberius. Tiberius' astrology sign was Scorpio, and this is reflected in the scorpion emblem of the Praetorians. They are organized in cohorts of 800 men each, stationed in a comfortable barracks on Rome's Viminal Hill. There is also a cavalry arm, the *equites singulares Augusti*.

The privilege of being a Praetorian would be justified if they were selected from the outstanding soldiers of the legions, but in fact most Praetorians are recruited as young men, and there is a very heavy bias for selecting Romans from Italy rather than the provinces. (However, the cavalry skills of Pannonians and Sarmatians means they have a much better chance if they apply for the *equites singulares Augusti*.) After completing their 16 years with the Praetorians, some of these soldiers move on to the regular legions where they take up commands as centurions, while others retire with a substantial bounty from the emperor as a farewell present. Transfers also take place the other way around, especially when the emperor Vitellius fired the entire Praetorian Guard for supporting his rival Otho in AD 69, and replaced them en masse with his own soldiers from the Rhineland legions.

✢ ✢ ✢

Gaius Vedennius Moderatus ... from Antium, legionary in XVI Gallica for ten years, transferred to the ninth Oraetorian cohort [of the Praetorians] and served there for eight years. Decorated twice, once by the Divine Vespasian, and by the emperor Domitian, Vanquisher of the Germans.

CIL 6. 2725 INSCRIPTION

✢ ✢ ✢

The best and most highly favoured Praetorians might go on to gain centurionates within the Praetorian Guard itself, and the top rank for a professional soldier is that of Praetorian prefect, commander of the imperial guard.

De Res Militari

Legionary cavalry are often used as couriers carrying orders or despatches.

✛

A courier on duty is recognized by a feather tied to his spear.

✛

Because a commander likes to report that his victories were achieved with minimal loss of Roman lives, there is always a temptation for him to get the auxilia to do the heavy fighting.

✛

An older auxiliary unit might distinguish itself from a newer one with the same name by adding the term *veteres* to its title.

✛

Praetorians on duty at the imperial palace wear togas.

✛ ✛ ✛

The auxiliaries led the advance, then came the foot archers, and after them four legions and the emperor himself with two Praetorian cohorts and the equites singulares [Augusti]. Then came other legions, horse bowmen and allied contingents.

TACITUS *ANNALS* 2.16

✛ ✛ ✛

✢ IV ✢

Legionary Kit and Equipment

huius de gladio memento, amici, viam ad hominis cor per viscera ferre *

Superb as Roman military equipment may be, the man who said you can never have enough of a good thing clearly never had to carry it, and carry it 20 miles a day, for weeks on end. A new recruit might like to remember this as he collects his equipment. 'Collect' is exactly the right word here, as legionaries buy their own kit, either from private sources or from the state. Essentially a legionary must have certain items of a particular type, and if he does not supply them himself, these will be provided, and the value extracted from his salary.

With this in mind, note that there is one item worth paying well over the odds to get exactly right, and this item is not a sword, shield or helmet. Some legions don't see action for decades, and there will be time to get the tools of offence and defence sorted out well before then. But peacetime or wartime, legionaries march a lot, and carry heavy packs while they are at it. Get the best footwear possible. Because proper footwear is so important, this overview of a legionary's equipment starts with the item on which Rome's military superiority is based – the *caliga*, the Roman soldier's sandal.

* With the sword, remember gentlemen, the way to a man's heart is through his stomach.

Caliga, caligula or *caligona*?

Checklist

1 Good fit – if new, allow for leather stretching.
2 Soft, well-worked leather.
3 Unbroken straps – make sure the skin-facing edges are smoothly bevelled.
4 New, well-fitting hobnails.

The late, unlamented emperor Caligula got his name because the general Germanicus, his father, used to dress him up as a miniature legionary. He became a mascot for the troops, who nicknamed him 'little boot'. (Or more precisely 'little military sandal'.) *Caligona* is a large sandal, and the standard issue footwear is a *caliga*.

Construction This vital piece of military equipment comes in three parts – a sole (for an ideal fit, check that the sole is about half a thumbnail smaller than the foot all round), an insole and an upper. The upper includes straps – *caligae fascentes* – to help with adjusting the fit. (It is these straps and the metal heavy studs on the sole that tend to wear out fastest and require most maintenance.) Check that the straps are closely double-stitched with waxed thread for maximum longevity.

Wear If the edges of the straps are not bevelled, borrow a small file and do this task for yourself. Hard edges definitely make themselves felt after the first few thousand steps. Remember also that leather stretches with use, so allow for some degree of expansion with new footwear. Those serving in a cold climate are happy to add heavy socks to avoid chilblains, but note that for really serious marching, socks are a nuisance. Fluid from burst blisters can dry and weld wool to raw skin, making the socks painful to walk in, and agony to take off.

Hobnails Good hobnails on the bottom of the *caligae* have the unexpected benefit of beefing up the wearer's kick on those occasions – e.g. crowd control, disagreements in taverns – where (mostly) non-lethal force is required. More conventionally, hobnails give the wearer excellent off-road traction on surfaces which may be slick with mud or blood. Hard, smooth surfaces are something of a problem. Consider the fate of the centurion Julian as he zealously followed up the enemy during the siege of Jerusalem:

He rushed amid the Jews as they scattered, and killed those that he caught ... but he was himself pursued by fate, which no mortal man can escape. Like all soldiers, he had shoes full of thick, sharp hobnails and when he ran on the pavement of the temple he slipped and fell down on his back with a great crash of armour. This made those running away turn back ... and strike at him with their spears and swords.

JOSEPHUS *THE JEWISH WAR* 6.8

✠ ✠ ✠

Tunic

Checklist

1 Well-made with tightly woven fabric.
2 Made of the right fibre (this varies according to unit or location).
3 Insist on an accompanying belt, and if possible, a securing pin.
4 If you can't get the same colour as the rest of the unit, choose white.

The legionary tunic sees a lot of wear, and many soldiers get through one every second month or so. This is a major expense, as even a cheap tunic costs around six denarii. (In fact, a soldier can expect his clothing bill to consume about a third of his pay.) A standard working tunic may be made of unbleached cloth, though most soldiers also have a walking-out tunic of purest white. Since these tunics are bleached white by a combination of urine and sulphur smoke, it is a good idea to air them well before wearing, lest they make an even more striking impression than intended.

Fit Tunics are definitely one-size-fits-all affairs, generally almost as wide as they are long. Raw recruits should remember that the military tunic is kirtled up above the knee, while civilians generally let theirs hang slightly lower. Select a tunic with a wide neck, since for heavy work it is a good idea to slip one arm through the neck hole and slide the right shoulder of the tunic under the arm, leaving the upper side of the body unencumbered by a baggy garment. In everyday use this wide neck hole can be closed by twisting it into a knot. This knot, held with an ornamental pin or two (*fibula*), makes a useful anchor for one's cloak.

The tunic, like the civilian model, is also a handy hold-all. A cord belt keeps it tight around the waist, and anything the wearer wants to carry is dropped down the neck for later retrieval.

Fabric The material of a tunic depends on location. Heavy wool is useful for Germania and Britannia, while those in warmer climes may prefer linen. Generally speaking, washing tunics is a communal activity, and it is a good idea to have the same material as the rest of the unit. Wool washes best if dunked in a large container and gently squeezed with paddles. It will suffer if treated as linen which is often whacked vigorously against rocks during cleaning.

✣ ✣ ✣

The weavers of the village are collectively to supply the required items for the soldiers in Cappadocia ... [including] tunic, white, with belt, 3 ¼ cubits [5 ft 1 in.] long, 3 cubits 4 dactuloi [4 ft 6 in.] wide, and weighing 3 minae [3 lb 6 oz] ... all of pure unstained wool with properly finished hems.

MILITARY CLOTHING ORDER DATED AD 138, SELECTED PAPYRI 395

✣ ✣ ✣

Colour The colour of any tunic will soon conform to the rest of the unit's, since dyes are not fixed and mingle promiscuously among all the clothes in the tub. Those units which like red dye for tunics do so because the dye – madder – is cheap and generally available. The macho reason for this preference is that it hides bloodstains, but first, legionaries are generally relaxed about the sight of blood (unless it is their own, in which case they tend to notice it whatever the tunic colour), and secondly, madder bleaches very quickly in the sun, so after a hard campaign the legion comes home clad in a rather fetching shade of pink. White is easiest to maintain and also shows up dirt well, which is important if on active duty, where the cleanliness of cloth can be a matter of life or death if fibres are driven into a wound.

Armour

Checklist

1 Good steel is vastly preferable to cheap iron.
2 Hooks, fastenings and attachments should have high-quality rivets.
3 Check for embedded rust – it can be the devil to get out.
4 Armour with dents panel-beaten back into shape is weaker armour.
5 Good fit is vital – get it personalized and all internal protrusions removed.

Type Having dealt with the essentials of footwear and tunics, we can move to less important issues such as armour. As every legionary knows, the main function of armour is to be polished, since it otherwise turns (almost overnight) an unmilitary shade of orange. Legionary armour may be chain mail or scale, but the most common type is the 'lobster-style', *lorica segmentata*, which consists of figure-hugging iron bands mounted on a leather frame. *Lorica segmentata* is stronger and lighter (and cheaper to make) than the chain mail generally worn by auxiliaries.

Maintenance Those with chain mail can clean their armour by putting it in barrels with a bit of sand and rolling the barrels to and fro while the links chafe themselves clean. *Lorica segmentata*, however, needs polishing with elbow grease, band by band by band. (There are 34 separate segments and various hinges as well, not to mention the tricky bits under the overlaps where no matter how well it is oiled, rust still gets in.)

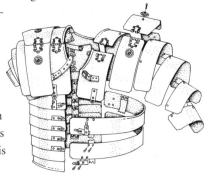

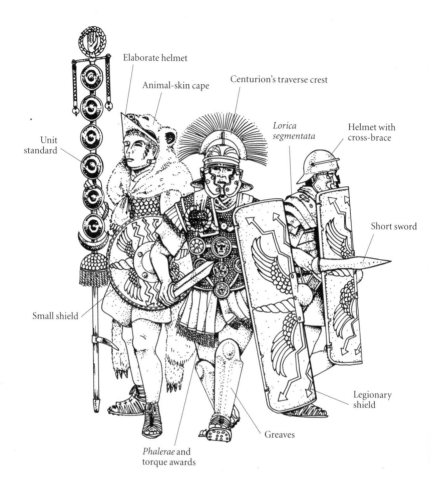

Elaborate helmet

Animal-skin cape

Centurion's traverse crest

Lorica segmentata

Helmet with cross-brace

Unit standard

Short sword

Small shield

Legionary shield

Greaves

Phalerae and torque awards

ABOVE *Elements of a Roman squad ready for action. From left to right we have a standard-bearer, a centurion and a standard legionary.*

OPPOSITE Lorica segmentata, *showing the breastplates, mid-collar plates, backplates, upper shoulderguard plates, lesser shoulderguard plates, hinged strap fittings, hinged and hingeless buckles, sub-lubate hinge halves and lower unit halves. There are variations on the basic design, but all types of this armour are light and flexible. But not simple or easy to maintain.*

Fit When donning this armour, the first thing to ensure is that you are wearing a scarf. Without one, the heavy chest band grinds into the top of the sternum while the wearer is marching and can break or even ulcerate the skin over time. Once the scarf is in place, the armour can be put on like a metal waistcoat, after which it is laced up in the front with leather ties. Well-fitting armour is both unobtrusive and flexible, so much so that it is easily forgiven its fiddly assembly and the tendency of fittings and hinges to snap at the wrong moment. In fact, a snapped hinge is a good opportunity to wheedle the armourer into readjusting the armour for an even better fit while he is making the repair.

Helmet

Checklist

1 Again, good fit is vital.
2 Do not pad to fit.
3 Find an up-to-date model.
4 Convex internal protrusions become concave indentations in the skull.
5 Gallic is best.
6 Consider weight-to-protection ratios.

Once bronze, helmets are now made of iron, and many soldiers still have a preference for those made in Gallic factories, believing the workmanship to be better than the Italian models. Helmets are a work in progress, and which one the new recruit gets depends on the model available.

ABOVE *Gallic helmet, contemporary design. This top-of-the-range model features a forehead cross-brace, decorative rivets and protective ear-ridges. Note the device on top for affixing plumes, and the loop on the wide neck-protector which allows the helmet to hang from your armour during the march.*

Construction All helmets have the same basic features. A reversed brim prevents any unpleasant surprises hitting the back of the neck, and the reinforcement across the forehead is to foil barbarian warriors who dream of cleaving their enemy's skull in twain with a single downward sweep. (Since the Dacians (p. 106) rather favour this technique and are armed accordingly, it may be worth seeking out a helmet with an extra iron cross-brace.)

The helmet has cheek flaps which may deflect missile weapons, but not a full-blooded sword swing, and the top should have a knob or some other way to attach plumes. Plumes were once highly fashionable in battle, but the later trend is to present the Roman army to its enemies as a no-nonsense killing machine (which it actually is), so plumes are restricted to certain types of parade.

Size Helmets are a case where size definitely matters. A tiny helmet perched on the top of the head is almost as ridiculous as an oversized helmet that tips forward over the eyes, and neither is likely to intimidate the enemy. It goes without saying that the ears should not be what holds the helmet above the eyebrows, but it is not a good idea to pad the helmet to fit.

Fit Any lining in the helmet should be both firm and not too thick. Too much soft padding will compress easily and will not protect the skull, since a solid blow will end up hitting the legionary very hard on the head with the inside of his own helmet. Seek out a helmet which both fits well and has the recent innovation of protective ridging above the ears, since otherwise the rim can chafe here and become a major distraction. In fact, it is a good idea to make sure that both the *lorica segmentata* and the helmet have as few internal protrusions as possible, since the wearer will get intimately acquainted with these after a few minutes of activity.

Helmets are heavy. If in a peaceful province, choose a helmet with minimal extra bracing. Despite this, the average legionary neck becomes several inches thicker after supporting that weight for a decade or so.

Shield showing unit insignia. The amount of battering a shield takes in combat demonstrates its protective value, but many a barbarian has learned too late that a properly handled Roman shield is a useful offensive weapon as well.

Shield (*scutum*)

Checklist

1 Get cover and shield as a matched pair.
2 Look for a durable – and water-resistant – paint job.
3 Check the type of wood carefully.
4 Avoid shields that have seen combat.
5 Check for strong metal reinforcement on the edges.

This particular item of kit spends most of its life inside the oiled goatskin cover made to hold it. The shield, carefully painted with the legion insignia, is only removed for maintenance, polishing, parades and battle. Being viciously curved means that the legionary shield makes a poor impromptu table or stretcher, both being how other nations and the auxilia employ what is otherwise a useless encumbrance until the moment one is actually under attack. (At which point it suddenly occurs to the legionary that in fact his shield is neither thick nor heavy enough.)

Construction During an attack, what a legionary actually holds between the spearpoints of the enemy and his own body is three layers of wood fitted in a precise pattern. Oak or birch are the preferred types of wood in these layers. Shield-makers favour birch, because it is bendy and easy to fit, and legionaries like oak for the same reason that shield-makers don't – it is close-grained and harder to cut through. In either case, the wood is made into plywood, and each layer is glued with the grain of the wood at right angles to the preceding layer. Wooden reinforcing strips are added to the back, and two small semicircles are cut through the wood in the centre of the shield, leaving a horizontal handle in between (some shieldmakers prefer to insert a metal bar here). On the enemy-facing side of the shield, the hole is covered by a metal plate with a round, bulging boss. The grip is held overhand, like a suitcase handle, so the shield can be brought sharply up into a defensive posture, or the carrier can punch with that hand, using his shield as the ultimate knuckleduster.

Colouring and identification Shields might be faced with fabric or thin leather. Leather is easier to clean, but if the decoration is in casein (a paint derived from milk), fabric holds the colours better. In either case, the shield needs regular waxing to keep the colours shiny and the wood in prime condition. Be sure to use a nail, punch or pointed chisel to hammer an identifying mark on your kit so as to avoid those little misunderstandings about ownership which arise in camp from time to time. The brass edging of the shield, or inside the boss are useful sites for such marks.

Size Not all shields are the same size or shape. In fact some of the old Augustan-style shields, with their slightly bowed edges, are still around. A recruit should choose himself a shield that protects from around the shoulder to the knee (about 35–45 inches), and which is just under 3 ft wide. Anything larger gets in the way of swordplay, and as the Roman army firmly believes, attack is the best form of defence.

*Scipio noticed that a certain shield had been elegantly and ornately
decorated, and said he was not surprised that it was so adorned,
in that the owner evidently trusted it more than his sword.*

FRONTINUS *STRATAGEMS* 4.5

✛ ✛ ✛

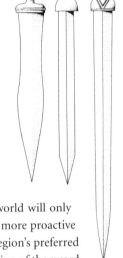

Three Roman swords. Getting a sword that is right for you might be the most important choice you ever make. The middle sword is the most contemporary, and the longer version on the right is no longer used by the infantry. However, auxiliaries and particularly cavalrymen favour this version.

Sword (*gladius*)

Checklist

1 Good balance.
2 High carbon steel is best.
3 Non-slip hand grips are life-savers.
4 Get sword and scabbard as a matched pair.

Useful as protection is, all the armour in the world will only delay the inevitable unless the wearer becomes more proactive in combat. To take the fight to the enemy, the legion's preferred technique is the up-close-and-personal application of the sword. Other sections of this text explain how to use the sword and what formation of legionaries makes that use most productive. At the moment we are concerned with the actual sword itself. Essentially speaking, a sword is a tool. In the case of a legionary sword, it is a tool carefully designed for intrusively penetrating the human body, preferably from the umbilicus to the heart via the organs in between.

Balance Beginners find the *gladius* unexpectedly heavy, and this is why anyone who intends to be swinging one around for a while needs to pay careful attention to the balance. Balance is important for two reasons. First, a well-balanced sword encourages a good 'sense of point', which is an intuitive and very important understanding of precisely where the tip of the sword is, even during situations where it is impossible to take the time to look and find out. Secondly, a balanced sword is less tiring to wield, which is important on those occasions when the fighting only stops if the enemy is dead.

Construction Basically a Roman sword is a sharp slab of metal, 18–22 in. long and about 2 in. wide. The sword is double-edged with a flattish diamond cross-section. Ideally, check with the armourer about the carbon density – most swords have low-carbon cores, but you should insist that at least the edges or preferably the entire exterior has a high carbon content, and is therefore better steel. Before a battle many legionaries obsessively put razor-like edges on the blade, but this is mainly a form of stress-relief. The actual work of a legionary sword is usually done with the point – it is a stabbing sword par excellence. Unusually for a stabber, there are no blood runnels; that is, grooves in the blade to let air into a wound. Without these runnels, flesh clamps around a blade and holds it in, so immediately after stabbing the sword needs a vicious twist to allow it to be withdrawn at once for re-employment elsewhere.

Fear struck their hearts. Being accustomed to fighting Greeks and Illyrians, they [the Macedonians] had seen wounds caused by spears arrows or occasionally by lances. But now they saw how the [Roman] gladius hispaniensis *cut arms off with the shoulder attached, severed heads from bodies cleanly at the neck, and bared internal organs through ghastly wounds – panic followed the realization of what kind of men and weapons they were up against.*

LIVY *HISTORY OF ROME* 31.35

Hand-grip A slippery grip on the handle is very dangerous for the reasons mentioned above, and especially as there is a high probability that the sword-wielder will have somewhat sweaty palms. Therefore, look for a well-balanced sword with a slightly rough grip. (Rawhide is better than wood, and bone is better than either.) Make sure that the tang (the part of the blade that goes back through the handle) is securely attached to the pommel. The pommel at the back of the sword is round and larger than with most swords, partly to better balance the weight of the sword, and partly because if the sword sticks in an opponent's flesh, the pommel gives good support for a backward pull.

Scabbard and fittings Only if a sword has the basics correct is it worth considering the other aspects, such as the decoration on the scabbard. Scabbards usually have brass plates with bas reliefs which are both ornamental and protective, and the leather covering of the scabbard is often decorated and embossed. The scabbard should be designed specifically for the sword it holds, so that it is neither so loose that the sword rattles (embarrassing during covert activities) or so tight that it binds (even more embarrassingly refuses to release the blade when it is urgently needed).

The overall product is slung over the shoulder on its own belt (baldric) to be worn high on the right side. Make sure the scabbard points slightly forward, or the sword will be difficult to draw and replace. Many legionaries like to be cross-belted, with the belt on the other side holding a *puglio*, the all-purpose dagger which, in day-to-day activity, sees a lot more use than the sword.

Spear (*pilum*)
Checklist

1 Except in battle, is it a useless, weighty encumbrance?
2 If yes, then it's a *pilum*.
3 All you need to look for is a chance not to carry one.

As any legionary knows, the *pilum* is no ordinary spear. The ordinary spear is used by people of many nationalities, including the Roman auxilia, but not by the legionary. On a long march, an ordinary spear is used in a number of ways. For a start, it is a handy walking staff. Secondly, stuck point first into the ground it provides an immediate pole, and three spears held with a leather string make an instant tripod (for hanging small game, such as rabbits). In the event of injury, put two spears longways inside a tunic and you have an instant stretcher. In combat, a spear is a medium distance missile weapon, but can be employed in close combat to give the user considerable reach. In less lethal situations it is a passable quarterstaff, and the quarterstaff is a weapon which many believe to be the best weapon a fighter on his own can possess. Yet for all its utilitarian applications, a spear is lighter than even a sword.

Drawbacks Almost all of these advantages, a legionary will bitterly point out, have been stripped away from the legionary spear – the *pilum*. The weapon starts off promisingly, with a solid 4 ft of ash wood on a slightly pointed base. But the balance of the spear is a solid triangle of wood on to which is riveted a shaft of about 2 ft 5 in. of thin, soft iron, which ends in a tiny triangular tip. This makes the *pilum* unconscionably heavy, and sometimes, just to make the weapon even heavier, a round lump of lead is added for good measure just before the metal shaft.

Since this thin shaft is iron, not steel, it bends very easily. Just to help with its fragility, one of the rivets fixing the shaft to the wood might be deliberately weakened. Because of this, the kind of hard usage which makes the ordinary spear a doughty companion on one's travels will instead turn the *pilum* into a sad, useless bit of droopy metal.

Advantages The standard spear is an all-purpose tool, whereas the *pilum* is a specialist. It is designed to be used once per battle (you can straighten a *pilum* out afterwards, but after a couple of bendings and straightenings the

Legionaries with field adaptations for the German winter. Note the toeless socks, short trousers under the tunics, the extra scarf and the fact that helmets are being worn rather than carried so as to protect the head from the elements.

metal breaks). The whole idea is that once a *pilum* has been thrown at the enemy it becomes useless, so there is no point (sometimes literally no point) in throwing it back. If a *pilum* hits a shield, its weight will force the shaft at least part of the way through. The rivet may well now break, and with the *pilum* embedded in it, the shield is little more than a hindrance to its bearer until he has got the *pilum* out of it. However, the *pilum* has arrived as part one of a legionary charge, and part two follows immediately afterwards, featuring the legionary himself, plus sword (and fully functional shield). Consequently there is seldom time for the *pilum*-extraction process. Generally, if a *pilum* hits a shield, the shield is best dumped, and the shield owner has to fight the legionary without it.

This does not mean that the *pilum* is designed mainly as a shield-removal tool, though it functions well as such. A well-thrown *pilum* is a killer. That hefty weight can drive the thin shaft right through a man's body, and since a unit of charging legionaries can throw their *pila* in perfect synchronization, one seldom has a single *pilum* to avoid, but (especially if you are unfortunate enough to be, for example, an enemy standard-bearer) up to a dozen at once.

It does not help the enemy that after carrying the formerly useless thing around for about a decade, when a legionary does get to throw his *pilum*, he hurls it from him with great force.

Other kit

There is a saying that if you have more possessions than you can carry for a mile, then these possessions actually own you. By this criterion, a Roman soldier on the march is a very free man. However, with just under 60 pounds on his shoulders, the average legionary might beg to differ. In the past a Roman army was followed by a baggage train and servants, and this train was as large – if not larger – than the actual fighting component of the army. This comfortable arrangement came to an end with general Marius (see p. 18), who decreed that instead of the soldiers' gear being carried by pack animals, the legionaries should carry it themselves, which is why legionaries are sometimes described as 'Marius' mules'.

Pack Legionaries do not carry packs with shoulder straps, not least because such packs are hard to dump in an emergency. Instead, apart from items actually carried on the body, everything is strapped to a *furca*. This is a pole some 4 ft long with a T shape formed by a crossbar. The pack (more of a rolled-up leather bag) is strapped to the crossbar.

Digging tool With the *furca* comes a *dolabra*, which is strapped to the main shaft. (The *dolabra* generally sees more use than sword, shield and *pilum* put together – see Chapter VIII for details).

Cloak Depending on the weather, the legionary's cloak may also be rolled into the pack. Cloaks are heavy, as they are generally made from wool. For best weatherproofing, this wool should still be steeped in the lanolin oil which kept the original sheep dry on a rainy hillside. Lanolin oil is somewhat aromatic, and is noticeable in a tent where eight men use their cloaks for bedding, but on the positive side, it is excellent for the skin.

Patera Another piece of kit that no legionary will voluntarily go without is his *patera*. This is an all purpose cup, cooking pot and food bowl. The best ones have a diameter of about 7 in., are made from bronze, sometimes lined inside with tin, and have grooves ground into them to help conduct heat during cooking. Because these often have to be put on the ground, select a *patera* with a wide, flat base rather than a rounded bottom. A heavy *patera* is more solid, and lasts longer, but weight is always a disadvantage on the march. So in selecting his *patera*, as so often in legionary life, a soldier must choose between two bad alternatives.

A good patera *is important. You might need to use your sword in anger only once or twice in a campaign, but you will need your* patera *two or three times a day.*

Water flask The water flask represents another such choice. A little-known attribute of water is that it is astonishingly heavy. Therefore a soldier must choose between carrying several pounds of water (depending on location) or risk the deprivations of thirst. In some regions, gourds, hollowed out and sealed with a wax stopper, make excellent lightweight water bottles. It is impossible to fix handles to these, but it is easy enough to fashion a net around the gourd and carry it on a sling.

Rations To this one should add several days' supply of food (including *buccellatum*, a kind of hard tack which is allegedly edible, lasts for years and could probably be used to patch shields).

With that lot on his back, a legionary is set to face the world. Naturally, he will have more possessions than this, both on the march and in camp (fortunately some items, including tents, are still carried by mules or ox-carts). Nevertheless, it is a good rule in any army that if you don't want to lose something, carry it with you.

✢ ✢ ✢

The infantryman is little more than a beast of burden.

JOSEPHUS *THE JEWISH WAR* 3.95

✢ ✢ ✢

De Res Militari

Vespasian once received a demand for boot-money from sailors who found that repeated marches from the port to Rome were wearing down their footwear. The notoriously stingy Vespasian responded by making the men march barefoot.

✢

A legionary might be humiliated for a minor infraction by being made to stand guard in an unbelted tunic.

✢

A set of *lorica segmentata* should weigh about 12–15 pounds – lighter armour means thinner plates and less protection, but makes marching less tiring.

✢

Some bronze helmets are still in service, but try to avoid these.

✢

Shields generally come out of combat in worse shape than any other kit, so need frequent repair or replacement.

✢

There is one mule for every eight men for the kit that is not carried on the person.

✢

A sword scabbard is called a *vagina*.

✢

The lanolin oil that waterproofs cloaks will be used in future skin-care products. Indeed the name of one famous brand is allegedly based on the word 'lanolin'.

OPPOSITE *Mess rations, one squad. On campaign the unit has a small grinder for corn, but in a hurry the corn can be boiled and eaten directly. Fresh vegetables are welcome, and any country boy in the squad knows how to set snares for a bit of wild hare to go with the meal.*

V

Training, Discipline and Ranks

si duo imperata inter se repugnantia simul tibi faciuntur, ambo sequere *

✛ ✛ ✛

Training

Training is done in roughly five graduated (rather than easy) stages, each of which is arranged so that just as a trainee believes he has just got past the worst, his instructors raise the bar to a whole new level.

1 Marching

'What use is a soldier to anyone', remarked the great general Scipio Africanus, 'if he cannot walk?' The army has taken this comment to heart, and one of the first thing a recruit learns is the terrain around his camp, as he walks over it, again and again. Once a squad of trainees can walk 20 miles in five hours, it's time to have a go at 40 miles in 12 hours. Once they can do that and still move the next day, it's time to start the 20 miles again, but this time in full armour. It is important to get used to the regular legionary step, as the Roman army likes to march in neat blocks and has little patience with stragglers. Marching is a large part of what defines a legionary (the remainder is mostly about looking good and killing people). Even after becoming fully trained and billeted in a stationary camp, a legionary can expect to go on frequent and lengthy training marches.

2 Combat by post

Once able to get to a fight – no matter how distant it may be – the legionary is taught what to do when he gets there. Weapons training is much the

---

* When you receive two contradictory orders, obey them both.

same as that given to gladiators. This is another innovation from the time of Marius, who, when promoted to general, discovered that soldiers trained by the gladiator instructors of his colleague, Rutilius Rufus, were generally superior to his own men. Therefore, like a gladiator in training, the first opponent every legionary faces is a large wooden post on which he practises swordplay. Sometimes this post is indoors, so that bad weather does not interfere with instruction, but generally the posts are outdoors, as most commanders feel that nothing relaxes a soldier more after training in bad weather than a few hours oiling and polishing his armour to keep it rust-free.

At least on such occasions the legionary's sword and shield remain tucked away from the elements. Training is done with a wooden shield and sword which will soon become more heartily hated than any Parthian or Dacian. These items are cunningly made much heavier than the standard kit so as to strengthen the legionary's arm as he hacks at the post for hour after hour, practising stabs, thrusts, feints and lunges. Though legionaries, as the later writer Vegetius remarks, 'laugh at those who use the edge [rather than the point] of the sword', the *gladius* is a well-balanced weapon and cuts are also included in the training repertoire.

3 Pilum *practice*

After adequate proficiency with the sword has been achieved, and a wooden post is no longer a fearsome opponent, it is time for *pilum* practice. As the ever-more cynical recruit is unsurprised to discover, the training *pilum* is heavier than the standard issue. Also, instead of a steel tip, the training *pilum* comes with a leather button on the end – solid enough to give a painful jab, but soft enough to leave no more than a bruise. This is because training with the *pilum* comes in two parts – how to throw it, and how to receive it. This is done by pairing squads of legionaries against each other, a process that will also become more familiar in sword practice as wooden posts are replaced by live humans. Again the weapons are padded, and the opponent is generally a fellow recruit, but on occasion the opponent may be a grinning veteran sadistically eager to show up any defects in the inexperienced fighter's technique, and to do the showing up as painfully as possible.

4 *Getting agile*

The importance of snugly fitting armour will now make itself apparent to those who have previously consider it unimportant. Being nimble is an important attribute in soldiers who are expected to climb scaling ladders and leap over ramparts in full armour. Therefore every barracks has a vaulting horse, which legionaries have to leap on or over in full armour. On these occasions expect any lumps or irregularities within the armour to be mirrored by purple bruises on the skin after every fall. As agility improves, the tasks get tougher, until the trainee is leaping the horse with an unsheathed sword and possibly also a *pilum* in his grasp. (By which time falls are even more undesirable.) On the bright side, those who show particular proficiency with the vaulting horse may get promoted to the real thing with a post in the legionary cavalry.

Each soldier practises daily with as much energy as if he were in battle.

JOSEPHUS *THE JEWISH WAR* 3.5

5 *Drill*

Having become a moderately proficient individual soldier, it is now time to move on to becoming a moderately proficient member of a unit. Drill follows drill, first on the parade ground and then in open country, until the unit's soldiers move like a single organism at a shouted command or trumpet blast. Each recruit learns his place in the formation, what to do if he ends up in the wrong place, how to change formation from a line to a wedge, or (Jupiter forbid!) if the line is broken, how to fall into a defensive circle, or fall back through lines of relieving troops without disordering them. Then the unit learns how to do all of the above while moving forwards, backwards or sideways at high speed over broken terrain. It is at this point that one fully appreciates the importance of having a helmet that allows the wearer to hear instructions instantly, since the slowest to react invariably becomes the focus of the trainer's 'special' attention.

Preparing for battle. These legionaries stand in full armour, shields at the ready, and though they are crammed together, shoulder-to-shoulder, this does not interfere with the combat ability of trained close-formation fighters.

The gain for the pain

After a particularly hard day, it may feel that the entire point of getting bruised, humiliated and exhausted has been simply to sate the sadistic inclinations of a particular instructor. And to be honest, that may well be the case. But this training is about more than getting fit while acquiring technical fighting skills. In future years, when fighting a desperate battle – perhaps without the prospect of rest, rations or reinforcements in the foreseeable future – you will be alongside legionaries who are accustomed to getting on with the job without sitting down and complaining about the injustice of it all. And of course, one can always fantasize that the instructor will be there too, casting uneasy glances over his shoulder at his vengeful former trainees every time the action gets heated.

This rigorous training instils the awareness of being a highly integrated cog in a very mobile killing machine. There is also the comforting knowledge that the part-time warriors on the opposing side have a fraction of a legionary's training, discipline and skills in manoeuvre. And even better, the enemy knows this too. In short, if as generally believed, morale is at least three times more important than physical numbers, good training means going into combat with the odds comfortably on your side.

I congratulate [the legionary legate] for having trained you in such a laudable manner.

HADRIAN TO LEGIO III AUGUSTA AD 128
INSCRIPTIONES LATINAE SELECTAE 2487

✣ ✣ ✣

Discipline, or decimation for beginners
The bad old days

Ah, the famous discipline of the Roman army! Campfire stories lovingly relate, in gruesome detail, the vicious punishments of martinets in the past. In the Samnite wars of 294 BC, when a unit broke and ran, the commander Atilius Regulus intercepted their flight with another block of infantry and cut down the fleeing men as deserters. Appius Claudius, ancestor of the emperor Tiberius Caesar, had clubbed to death every tenth man (hence the term 'decimation') in a unit that fled from battle. Another general, Aquilius, did the same, though he opted for beheading. Crassus the triumvir decimated soldiers of a unit that ran away from the rebel gladiators of Spartacus, and when not wooing Cleopatra, Mark Antony executed every tenth man of two cohorts who had allowed the enemy to set fire to his siege works. In AD 18 soldiers of III Augusta were decimated by *fustuarium* (see below) after running from Numidians in Africa. In Republican times the general Metellus Macedonicus in Spain set the tone. When his soldiers were driven from a strongpoint by the enemy, he gave the survivors time to make their wills before sending them to re-take the position, telling them that they would not be allowed back into the camp until they had done so.

The legionaries strike back

One of the things to note about these draconian punishments is that they mostly belong in the past, in the days before the professional army (though the last decimation was by the emperor Galba in AD 69). Even in olden times the army did not necessarily take its medicine quietly. Also in Spain, the commander Servilius Galba – an ancestor of the emperor Galba, as it happens – decided to punish his cavalry for making rude jokes about him by sending them to gather firewood on a hill known to be infested with the enemy. Outraged, many of the other soldiers voluntarily joined in the firewood detail, and their numbers kept the enemy at bay. On their return, the soldiers stacked the wood around their commander's tent, and set fire to it.

Nor is the professional army immune from fits of unprofessional conduct:

✢ ✢ ✢

In a blind frenzy of rage, they fell with drawn swords upon the centurions, whom soldiers have resented from time immemorial, and who had first provoked their savage fury. They threw them to the ground and beat them ferociously ... the mangled and sometimes lifeless bodies were thrown out of the fortifications into the river Rhine.

TACITUS *ANNALS* 1.32

✢ ✢ ✢

This charming little anecdote is worth quoting to oneself after a centurion has been particularly difficult.

What to expect

Despite these gruesome stories, the reality is that the degree of difficulty one has with military discipline varies wildly depending on location and commander. Some older legionaries can still remember tales of life in the eastern legions before the Parthians became bothersome.

*It was well known that the army contained veterans who had never
stood guard duty or a night patrol, soldiers who had neither helmets
or breastplates. Instead they were sleek and wealthy businessmen
who spent all their time in towns, and to whom ramparts and ditches
were strange novelties.*

TACITUS *ANNALS* 13.35

✛ ✛ ✛

It is not often that life gets quite so good for a legionary. Indeed, an easy-going commander is not necessarily good news if he allows the centurions to become vicious in their bribe-taking (see Life in Camp p. 115), whereas a disciplinarian who sticks to the rules is actually good news for a soldier who does the same. Not all punishments are applied with the same severity at all times, and considerable leniency is given to first offenders. What might earn a severe beating in one time and place might amount to no more than a strict talking-to in another.

Punishments

Here, in ascending order, is a list of punishments that lie in wait during a legionary's life. Consider the minor ones unavoidable, the collective punishments unfortunate, and remember that no legionary commits serious infringements or grossly neglects his duty twice, as he is executed the first time.

Minor punishments – generally inescapable

Castigato This may be no more than a casual whack from the *vitis*, the vine-wood staff which the centurion carries for this purpose, or it may be a serious beating with the same stick. (One of the above-mentioned centurions thrown into the Rhine in AD 14 had the nickname 'Get-me-another', as he generally got through more than one stick per beating.)

Pecunaria multo Getting pay docked – very common for losing equipment (no matter how) or riotous conduct involving locals, with the deductions going to pay for the damage.

Munerum indictio Getting extra duties, often involving stables or latrines. This is often readily converted into *pecunaria multo* by bribing the appropriate centurion, and in fact there is often a strong suspicion that the centurion has given the punishment precisely to get this bribe. Sometimes these duties have to be performed in a humiliating way – a favourite being standing guard with the tunic unbelted like a woman's dress.

The above covers most minor offences in day-to-day life. More serious crimes or derelictions of duty result in the authorities getting correspondingly nastier.

Major punishments – to be avoided!

Militiae mutatio Involves losing either rank or long-service privileges, and as these are earned through long and often painful experience, their loss is bitterly felt. *Gradus deiectio* involves the same deprivations, but is combined with transfer to an inferior unit.

Animadversio fustium This is a flogging – not a few whacks from a centurion, but a serious flogging carried out before the entire unit. This is for major derelictions such as falling asleep on guard duty in camp. (Propping up the shield with a *pilum* and snoozing while leaning on the shield can result in a revealing and thunderous crash if the snoozer falls so deeply asleep that the entire unstable tripod collapses.)

Fustuarium Guards caught asleep in camp have a painful future. Guards caught sleeping while the army is in the field have no future. They are beaten to death. This happens after a trial before the leading officers of the camp – at least a military tribune. Once sentence has been passed, the tribune lightly taps the condemned man with his staff and steps back. Then it is up to his fellow soldiers to kick beat, flog or stone their victim to death. Often, given the dangers of a night attack on the camp, this is done with great enthusiasm, but some very popular soldiers get off with a severe mauling that leaves them crippled for life.

Collective punishments (in order of severity):

Frumentum mutatum *Frumentum* is the daily food ration. A unit in disgrace loses all meat from its diet, and is switched from wheat to barley rations. As barley is usually used as animal fodder, this represents a substantial loss of status. Occasionally the commanding officer adds insult to injury by docking the pay of those in the unit at the same time.

Extra muros This is a punishment by which a unit is sentenced to pitch tents outside the walls of the legionary camp. Even when in friendly territory and mild weather, this is a keenly felt exclusion from the only community the legionary knows. A host of minor punishments can be expected to accompany the large communal one. When a unit is decimated, the remainder of the unit generally end up outside the walls, and often have to remain there until they have shown conspicuously suicidal heroism against the enemy.

Misso ignominosa This is when the emperor simply decides that a unit is too useless to be part of the Roman army. Its members – sometimes an entire legion – are told to go away in disgrace and spend the rest of their lives living down the shame. They lose their pensions. Note that *misso ignominosa* can also be applied to selected individuals.

When he [the general Germanicus] asked what had become of the discipline that was their glory in days of old, they [the soldiers] laughed bitterly and showed him their bodies marked and scarred by the lash.

TACITUS *ANNALS* 1.35

✢ ✢ ✢

Ranks: from bottom to top

This is a somewhat misleading term. The Roman army does not offer legionaries a career path as such. The vast majority who join the ranks leave with the same status 25 years later. Those wanting to become centurions might be promoted from the ranks for outstanding conduct, but more probably purchase those positions with cash or influence before they sign up. The higher ranks – the legionary legate and the military tribunes who share his tent – are political appointees who are doing their military duty before going on to higher things.

But this is not to say that all legionaries are equal. Some are more equal than others, and any ambitious legionary will work fast to put distance between himself and the common herd.

Munifex A recruit can expect to start as a *munifex*. The *munifex* is a soldier with absolutely no rank or privileges. It is not even the bottom rung of the legionary career ladder – it is the bit they rest the ladder on. If you are a *munifex*, the donkey carrying the troop's tent probably outranks you.

Immunis Once signed up and fully trained, the first objective is to become an *immunis*. Legionaries fall into two categories, those who have special responsibilities – the *immunes* – and those who do not. The non-specialists are the hewers of wood and the carriers of water, available for unpleasant tasks such as latrine duty and heavy-duty lifting. Those immune from such drudgery have their own particular tasks, be they working in the smithy or doing the legion accounts. An *immunis* is still a *miles gregarius*, a common soldier, but life is generally somewhat easier, as is shown by the fact that an *immunis* may be punished by having this status stripped away for misbehaviour.

If aspiring to become an *immunis* – and one should – it is a good idea to become proficient at a trade such as plumbing, weapon-making or carpentry. Being literate is a huge advantage, as the legion always needs clerks for correspondence and record-keeping. Anyone able to read or write should make this fact known at once to the *cornicularis*, the trumpeter, who is usually also in charge of the legion's clerks. One of the advantages of clerking is that it is usually done indoors. Admittedly this is to protect the writing materials rather than the human, but the clerk gets the benefit nevertheless. A particularly numerate individual may become a *signifer*, the man who carries the legion standard (not the eagle – this is the job of the even more senior *aquilifer*). The *signifer* carries the 'open hand' emblem reminding soldiers of their oath, and is also in charge of the legionaries' retirement fund. Why pensions are entrusted to a man who becomes a javelin magnet in combat becomes less of a mystery when you realize that legionaries will fight desperately to defend the standards – partly because they are also protecting the man who knows the exact status of their pension.

At this time an *immunis* is not a rank, or even an official status. If a bloody-minded centurion puts an *immunis* on to ditch-digging detail, there is nothing that individual can do but grit his teeth and hope that his specialist contribution to the welfare of the legion will be missed by someone important enough to get him back to his proper duty.

Those to be freed from [other] duties ... The waggon-repairer, the tribune's orderly and Curiatius and Aurelius, the bookkeeper and clerk.

FROM THE DUTY ROSTER OF AN EGYPTIAN LEGION (EITHER III CYRENAICA OR XXII DEIOTARIANA) PAPYRUS GENEVE LAT. 1.4.B

Standard bearer as seen in later ages. Carrying the standard of his unit was among the most senior positions available to the common legionary. A standard bearer can expect to have a large amount of the enemy's attention dedicated to him personally during a battle, and needs to be the intrepid and steely-jawed kind of character depicted here. Carrying the eagle on the march is no easy task either, so think hard whether the job is worth the prestige and double pay.

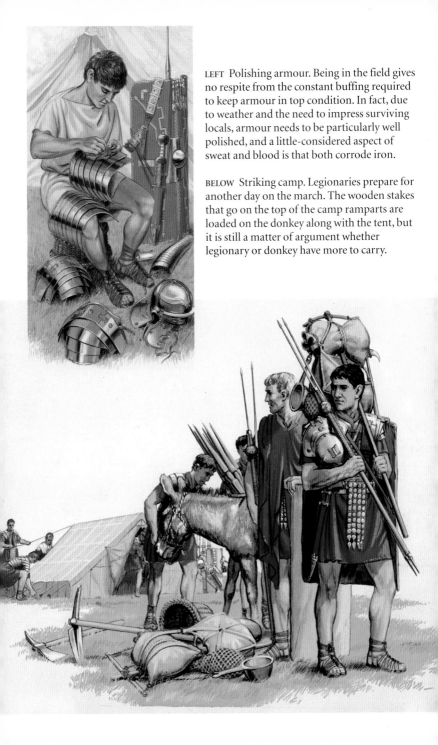

LEFT Polishing armour. Being in the field gives no respite from the constant buffing required to keep armour in top condition. In fact, due to weather and the need to impress surviving locals, armour needs to be particularly well polished, and a little-considered aspect of sweat and blood is that both corrode iron.

BELOW Striking camp. Legionaries prepare for another day on the march. The wooden stakes that go on the top of the camp ramparts are loaded on the donkey along with the tent, but it is still a matter of argument whether legionary or donkey have more to carry.

OPPOSITE ABOVE 'Take that, you wooden post, you!' A legionary practises combat drills until they become automatic reflexes while his comrades hurl button-tipped *pila* in the background.

TOP A centurion chastises a soldier for an offence while on the march. Since the legionary has armour beneath his cloak, the stick is not threatening, but the centurion has plenty of other punishments in reserve.

ABOVE About four per cent of Rome's military might – i.e. one legion, drawn up in parade formation. Note the double-strength first cohort on the left with *aquilifer* and standard bearers in front, and the legionary cavalry on the right.

ABOVE Then and now. On the left legionaries and their centurion take on an attack of *falx*-wielding Dacians, their right arms strengthened by an armoured sleeve.

OPPOSITE BELOW Next the legionaries launch their *pila* as they surge into a counter-attack. Note the lead weights behind the shaft which give the *pilum* extra heft.

ABOVE The good old days. Caesar's legionaries during a siege assault. The helmets have plumes, the shields are rounder, but the barbarians are every bit as hairy.

ABOVE LEFT Roman cavalry deploy into battle formation. During a pitched battle the cavalry spend much of the time in reserve. Horses tire quickly, and will be needed either to follow up a victory or cover a retreat depending on the fortunes of the day.

ABOVE Every cavalryman's fantasy. After the battle, the cavalry follow up the fleeing enemy and crush them beneath the horses' hooves. It's the moment that these cavalrymen will probably want immortalized on their tombstones.

LEFT Romans take time out from fighting Hannibal to dig the ramparts of a camp while their comrades stand guard. Three hundred years later little has changed, and the centurion inspecting the earthworks still is not satisfied.

ABOVE Ditch digging in AD 100. The armour is different, but it is still topsoil, and the centurion is still complaining bitterly about the quality of the spadework.

BELOW Legionary camp of XVI Gallica at Novaesium (Neuss) on the Lower Rhine in AD 43, view from the Decumanian gate. Today XVI is Legio XVI Flavia Firma, and would prefer its inglorious days on the Rhine to be forgotten.

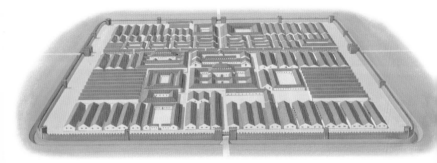

Principalis Those without particular skills other than being good soldiers should aspire to becoming a *principalis*. This is even better than being an *immunis*, but is open to correspondingly fewer legionaries. A *tesserarius* is an example of a *principalis*. As his name suggests, he is one of those in charge of organizing the sentry duties (the watchword for the day is usually written on a pot sherd, or *tessera*). Also among the *principales* is the *optio*, a man designated to take over the responsibilities of the centurion should the centurion be unavailable due to his other duties or because he has a spear embedded in his chest. The *optiones* of a legion have their own guild (*schola*), and with the other *principales*, form a tightly knit clique. *Principales* have the best chance of becoming centurions, with whom they work closely in any case. Once a legionary has got his *caliga* into the door of this little club, the remaining years of his service are almost guaranteed to go smoothly.

Centurions and other officers

A legionary has little interaction with the top brass of the legion. A good basic rule is to avoid anyone with a transverse helmet crest or a pretty ribbon tied under the pectorals of his breastplate. The ribbons designate officers, and about the best that can be said for these men is that they do their share of fighting, and die at the same rate as ordinary soldiers. Centurions too are expected to show inspiring valour, and as their distinctive crests make them conspicuous targets, the enemy kill them in goodly numbers – a fact which causes most legionaries little distress ...

The non-legionary ranks
Centurion

Centurions have a complicated and incestuous hierarchy of ranks, which seem mainly concerned with who is entitled to the best seat in the tavern or is the last to conduct a fatigue party out into the rain. There are some 60 centurions in a legion – which any soldier will tell you is far too many – and the centurions of the first cohort look down on the centurions of the other cohorts, though a centurion of the front rank (*pilus prior*) might look down on a centurion of the back rank (*pilus posterior*).

Whether a *pilus hastatus prior* (the names relate to their places in the order of battle) of the third cohort is superior to a *pilus principes prior* of the fifth cohort may be of great concern to the two men in question, but not much to anyone else. To the average legionary, all centurions are *dolori posteriori* (pains in the backside) and are most appreciated when they are away on detached duty, which is often the case. Centurions have a mix of initiative and rank which makes them the army's all-purpose soldiers, suitable for conducting diplomatic missions, judicious executions, escorting important prisoners or leading detachments of soldiers on raids, reconnaissance or rear-guard actions.

-- -- -- -- -- -- -- -- -- --

Centurion proudly displaying the distinctive transverse crest on his helmet. On his armour he displays the torque and phalerae *awarded for bravery in battle, and in one hand he carries the* vitis, *his vine-stick for whacking legionaries.*

✝ ✝ ✝

*In that legion there were two very brave men ... centurions T. Pullo and
L. Vorenus. There used to be continual disputes between them.*

CAESAR *GALLIC WAR* 5.44

✝ ✝ ✝

Primus Pilus The leading centurion of the legion. He will have got there
through skill at military fighting and political infighting. His main quali-
ties are courage, ruthlessness, high organizational ability and a low level of
compassion. He may be respected, is almost certainly feared, and is generally unloved.

Military tribunes

Ignore comments such as 'if anyone ever saluted a military tribune, the
light must have been bad'. It is true that in the past some of these wannabe
generals joined the army simply to further their political careers, and have
occasionally been known to go to pieces on hearing that the enemy is
approaching. However, in the modern army most tribunes come with
experience of command in an auxiliary unit and can throw a cohort or two
around the battlefield with reassuring professionalism. There are five of
these tribunes per legion. Their competence varies, but their ambition is
invariably naked and shark-like in its intensity.

Praefectus castrorum

The prefect of the camp. While the other officers may or may not know
their jobs, the *praefectus* is a professional to the bone. He is usually the
longest-serving centurion in the legion, and knows far more about its
history and operation than anyone else. Fortunately he outranks the military tribunes, and it is a very self-confident *tribunus laticlavus* who will go
against his advice. The *praefectus* is also about the only man who can take a
primus pilus aside and give him a spot of advice, or a talking-to if required
(he would have been a *primus* himself before promotion).

Tribunus laticlavus

Should anything unfortunate happen to the legate (such as being recalled to Rome and executed as a potential traitor) the *tribunus laticlavus* will take over. The 'laticlavus' is a reference to the broad stripe worn on this individual's toga, since, like his commander, this officer is theoretically a senator, or at least of senatorial class. However, legion commands are starting to go to non-senators, a sign of either declining standards of public life or of a more professional army, according to one's viewpoint. Expect a fresh-faced young man who will be constantly asking the *praefectus castrorum* what he is supposed to be doing.

Legionary legate

The top man. If the legion is the only one in a province, he will probably also be the provincial governor. The average legionary legate spends only three to four years in charge, as emperors don't like legionaries to become too attached to their commanders. After all, commanding a significant percentage of Rome's entire military power can give a man ideas.

Over the next nine years I was in charge of the cavalry and [then] commander of a legion.

THE HISTORIAN VELLIUS PATERCULUS GIVES HIS
MILITARY CREDENTIALS. *VEL. PAT.* 2.104

When some of the military tribunes had been slain by the enemy, the praefectus castrorum *surrounded ... many centurions injured and some front rank centurions killed, the valour of the common soldiers gained glory, by ... winning a desperate victory.*

CAMPAIGNING IN ILLYRIA AD 9 *VEL. PAT* 2.112

De Res Militari

Good earthworks and ramparts are important. Even after he has completed basic training, a legionary is expected to spend several hours a week refining his skills at combat – and at ditch-digging.

✛

During the Rhine mutinies, after they had disposed of the centurions, the legionaries organized and carried out their own sentry duties, patrols and the everyday running of the camp.

✛

A Roman 'step' is a double pace, from when one foot leaves the ground to when it hits it once more. A thousand such paces (*mille*) make a Roman mile of 1,620 yards, or 140 yards shorter than the 21st-century version.

✛

The Roman army has two marching speeds. The 'military pace' is a brisk 4.5 miles per hour used for manoeuvring in a hurry. Marching pace is a longer, easier stride.

✛

Among the extraordinary tasks entrusted to centurions were the bringing of St Paul to Rome and the killing of Agrippina, the mother of the emperor Nero.

✛

Promotion to centurion is at the recommendation of the legate to the governor and is approved by the emperor.

✛

From tent-makers to surveyor's clerks, the legion has at least 20 specialist roles which are filled by the *immunes*.

VI

People Who Will Want to Kill You

feminas semper molliter tracta, si ab earum viris forsitan apprehendaris *

Ompne of the joys of serving with the Roman army is that the enemy comes in a huge variety of guises. Just as you have become accustomed to dealing with naked German tribesmen leaping out of ambush and stabbing away with fire-hardened pointy sticks (which is harder to deal with than it sounds), a transfer can bring you against Parthian cavalrymen with levelled lances riding knee-to-knee, armoured from their toes to their impassive iron face masks, thundering down in their serried hundreds. Whether dealing with a chariot charge by blue-painted Picts in the Caledonian snows, an unexpected dagger thrust from a *sicarius* in a Jerusalem tavern, or a storm of javelins coming out of an African dust cloud stuffed with Numidian horsemen, the more a legionary knows about his foes, the better his chances of surviving them. Here are some enemies an unprepared legionary may meet during the final seconds of his career.

The Picts – death in the mist

Briefing

South of the border, the Britons are pacified, if 'pacified' is the right description for a surly populace who pass their lives under lowering grey skies, and require more legionaries per head to keep them under control than anywhere else in the empire. (Britain has three legions – the larger and more populous Hispania has one.) Those who have been north will know

---

* Always be nice to the women if there is any chance of being captured by their men.

both the Pict and the thistle – small, purple-blue, prickly, and liable to suddenly stab the unwary. Those living just south of the border might not see the Picts, but will be able to infer their presence from the way that entire flocks of sheep vanish mysteriously overnight.

The red hair and large limbs of the inhabitants of Caledonia point clearly to a German origin ... even the Gauls were once renowned in war; but ... they lost their courage along with their freedom. This too has happened to the long-conquered tribes of Britain; the rest are still what the Gauls once were.

TACITUS *AGRICOLA* 11

The name 'Pict' is soldiers' slang for any northern Briton, and 'Pict' has the same origin as the word 'picture', as both are painted. In the case of the Picts the colouration comes not only from their plentiful tattoos, but also from the woad with which they slather themselves before going into battle. Not only does the combination of woadish blue and pictish red hair induce

Weapons swing into action as another high-speed Pictish ambush charges from cover down the hillside of a Caledonian glen to ruin the day of an unsuspecting Roman patrol.

nausea in enemies unused to the colour clash, but the woad is an antiseptic which helps to prevent wounds becoming infected. Caledonians make up the majority of the Picts, but recently the mix has been enriched by a few blonde Britons unable to stomach Roman rule who have made their homes in the north.

Combat techniques

A tribal people, the Picts are engaged in busy internecine combat when not taking on the Romans. When pressed they retire to hill forts which they defend very competently. Unless these forts are surrounded with large numbers of very alert sentries, those legionaries making a dawn assault may find that the enemy has melted away in the night and is currently looting the Roman supply train back down in the valley.

This tactic of 'disperse and concentrate elsewhere' was used in the AD 80s in a night attack on the unfortunate Ninth Legion. It was so effective that the Picts might have wiped the legion out had the cavalry not come riding to the rescue. The soldiers of the Ninth had just got over a similar mauling by Boudicca, so blue is not their favourite colour.

The Romans fought a massive battle against the Picts and their allies in the north of Caledonia at a place called Mons Graupius in AD 84. After their victory, the Romans found to their frustration that some 20,000 of the enemy had melted into the landscape, and scouts could not even find them, let alone bring them back to battle. These men, and their children, are still out there, and still unconquered. Many a forage party has found the Picts appearing like wraiths from the mist, and later patrols have found those same foragers, some of them still in quite large pieces.

✛ ✛ ✛

To us who live on the furthest borders of the earth and of freedom, this remote sanctuary of Britain's glory has until now been a defence ... So let us, a fresh and unconquered people, show right from the very first engagement what heroes Caledonia has.

THE BRITISH LEADER GALGACUS BEFORE MONS GRAUPIUS,
TACITUS *AGRICOLA* 30FF

✛ ✛ ✛

Summary

You might think that warriors who fight with only a laughable pretence at discipline and co-ordination, using only spears and crude shields (though important warriors have swords and even imported or looted armour) are not serious opposition. And indeed, when it comes to an armed confrontation the Picts can be beaten, as they were at Mons Graupius, by auxiliaries alone. But so ferocious is their guerrilla campaign that there is talk of withdrawing from the north altogether, building a wall from one side of the island to the other, and pretending that Caledonia does not exist. The legionary garrison at the northern fort of Inchtuthil has already been withdrawn, and the abandonment of auxiliary bases proceeds apace.

Notes

1 Just because you can't see them it does not mean they are not there.
2 When you do see them it may well be too late.
3 Conquering Picts is easy. Getting them to understand that they are conquered is apparently impossible.
4 Fighting Picts also involves fighting fogs, cold and long, damp winters that grow mould over tunics and between the toes.

Germans – Teutonic fury

✝ ✝ ✝

*The Germans who combine immense ferocity with a degree of cunning
that seems incredible to someone who has no experience with this
race of born liars ...*

VELLEIUS PATERCULUS *HISTORY OF ROME* 2.118

✝ ✝ ✝

Briefing

Ask an experienced legionary from the Rhineland (say, a veteran from XXII Primigenia) what it is like to fight Germans, and the answer will probably be a patient sigh, and the question, 'which Germans?' Apparently to the connoisseur, Germans – though invariably large, hairy and ferocious –

German warrior in an unwontedly pensive attitude. This particular specimen is relatively well-off as he has both a well-made shield and iron points on his spears. Germans have the disconcerting ability to change abruptly from placid tribesmen to screaming, bloodthirsty, tattooed nightmares.

come in a variety of flavours. Some Germans, for example the Frisians, Cherusci or Chatti, may not like the Romans very much, but over a century of rubbing along with them has induced a certain degree of Romanization. While your average tribesman still likes quaffing beer in large amounts, he will have also developed a taste for wine, and German leaders might even be able to comment knowledgeably on the vintage.

✢ ✢ ✢

... the other German tribes; I mean the Cherusci, the Chatti, the Gamabrivii and the Chattuarii, and also, near the ocean, the Sugambri, the Chaubi, the Bructeri and the Cimbri, and also the Cauci, the Caülci, the Campsiani and several others.

STRABO *GEOGRAPHY* 7.3

✢ ✢ ✢

Such warriors have also decades of experience at fighting the legionaries, and indeed, some of their most cunning leaders – Arminius and Civilis, for example – had served with the same legionaries against whom they later turned their military talents. These men have learned that blind aggression is no match for a well-hurled *pilum*, and that while legionaries will slaughter Germans in the open field, the Germans have the edge in thick and preferably boggy forest. (Germany has a depressing amount of bog and forest.) A semi-Romanized German knows his armour, and may be expert with a sword. He is capable of ingenious insults in Latin, or even, if he senses disaffection among the legions he is fighting, of shouting job offers to anyone who wants to switch sides.

The barbarians were adapting themselves to Roman ways, becoming accustomed to hold markets, and meeting in peaceful assemblies. Under careful [Roman] supervision they were forgetting their old customs gradually and without really noticing. Because of this they were not disturbed by their changing lifestyle, and were becoming different without knowing it.

CASSIUS DIO *HISTORIES* 56.18

✛ ✛ ✛

Combat techniques

To fight the original Germanic warrior, one has to go north or east. Peoples like the Semnones or the Quadi still go into battle with a minimum of clothing and carrying only the *framea*, the dreaded Germanic battle spear. What their battle tactics lack in subtlety is compensated for by rabidly enthusiastic blood-lust, and the lack of sophisticated equipment is made up for with numbers. The usual battle tactic is to pack a huge mass of warriors into a tight wedge, with the better-armoured types on the outside, and hurtle at great speed into the Roman lines. This *furor Teutonicus* – the savage German battle charge – apparently has to be experienced to be fully appreciated, though if the charge does manage to break the line, appreciation is not even the last thing that the legionary will feel during his remaining moments.

If the charge is broken, the Germans will not usually hang around for another try, but vanish into the woods as unexpectedly as they arrived. The legionaries will then examine the bodies of the fallen, and perhaps note the distinctive top-knot hairstyle of the Suebic tribes, or pull the nasty throwing axes of the Franks out of their shields. If this is a sudden attack, note the well-armoured gent with a muscular bodyguard. He is the chieftain, and if the attack fails he will lead his men back to the forest. Kill him, and his retinue will fight to the death, since they are vowed to fight and die with him, and there is nothing for them back home if they break their oath.

If the attack succeeds, it may well be a good idea for the legionaries to fight to the death as well. The Germans are not very gentle with their prisoners, and practise human sacrifice in a particularly messy and painful form.

Summary

The good thing about the average German is that he is lazy, disorganized and undisciplined, unlike the efficient, industrious and well-drilled Italians. It has been found that by and large, Germans like to fight each other as much as they enjoy killing Romans. Many an attack on the Roman lines (called *limes*, or 'limits' in these parts) has been foiled by delivering a waggon-load of wine to one set of enemies in return for their falling upon another set. 'Divide and conquer' is a time-honoured Roman tactic, and it works particularly well in the Rhinelands.

Notes

1 Avoid bogs and forests. This basically involves staying out of Germania.
2 The most ferocious part of a German attack is over in four minutes. The trick is to be still alive after five minutes.
3 If you can avoid fighting the Germans for long enough, they will fight each other instead.
4 The same generals who affect to despise the Germans as soldiers leap at the chance to hire them as mercenaries.

The Jews – asymmetric resistance as an art form

Of all the many enemies who might try to kill you, only the Jews are able to sue you if they fail. But the Jewish people have the advantage of being citizens of Rome's empire, though they themselves do not see things quite that way. Incorporated as a province two generations ago, the proud and stubborn people of Judaea showed their appreciation in AD 66 with a rebellion that wiped out most of Legion XII at Beth Horon, and captured its eagle.

Jewish resistance fighters. One advantage of Judaea being a Roman province is that you will understand most of the insults being hurled at you, of which Romani ite domum *is likely to be among the least cruel and hurtful.*

Briefing

Although the rebellion was quashed by the future emperor Vespasian, and Jerusalem was largely flattened in the siege and sack led by Vespasian's son Titus, the Jewish people can hardly be said to have been crushed by defeat. Their resistance is both outside the law, and through the law. The Jewish people have a long tradition of rabbinical study, and many know their own and imperial legislation backwards. The result is a regular stream of embassies to the emperor giving chapter and verse of real and imagined injustices, while a large and active guerrilla population simultaneously harasses the army in the countryside. Another full-scale rebellion is almost a certainty within the next generation or so.

The term *listim* pops up frequently in this context. Depending on one's viewpoint, *listim* are politicized bandits, guerrillas or terrorists. The rabbis, meanwhile, use the same term to refer to the Roman authorities, so all that can be said with certainty is that the term is not a compliment.

A major problem for legionaries is distinguishing Jewish friends from foes – and this problem is not limited to Judaea. There are large and mutinous Jewish populations in Cyreniaca, Alexandria and Cyprus. (As well as 50,000 or so of their better-behaved compatriots in Rome.)

On the one hand, there are those such as Flavius Josephus, a rebel leader who threw in his lot with the Romans and spent the rest of his life trying to bridge the gap between the two cultures. There is also a rabbinic group in favour of accommodation with the Romans, not least because fighting the Romans keeps the Jews from fighting each other.

✢ ✢ ✢

[Jews] should pray for the peace of the government; for, except for the fear of that, we should have swallowed each other alive.

ETHICS OF THE FATHERS (*MISHNAH*) 3.2

✢ ✢ ✢

Resistance types and techniques

On the other hand there are Maccabees, those Jewish peoples following the long Jewish tradition of resisting invaders (the Assyrians, Persians and Seleucids had similar problems with the Jews). The Zealots are a faction who take this view one step further and consider armed resistance a duty. The Sicarii are resistance fighters who consider the Zealots weak and wimpish, in that the Zealots do not practise the Sicarii traditions of wholesale assassination, kidnapping and extortion, not only of Romans but of any Jews who are insufficiently enthusiastic about their cause.

✢ ✢ ✢

For the Jews deemed it intolerable that foreigners should make their homes in their city and that foreign religious rites should take root there.

CASSIUS DIO *HISTORIES* 69.12

✢ ✢ ✢

Overall, life with a hostile Jewish community tends not to be dull. Those training *pila* are occasionally called into play for crowd control, but use of even blunted spears, or the throwing of these with particular enthusiasm, leads to a delegation to the governor complaining about 'excessive force'. Because when they do rebel, the Jews fight like men possessed, the emperors tend to take their sensibilities seriously. One legionary, for example, was executed for insultingly lifting his tunic to expose himself to the Jewish people, and of all the subjects of the emperor only the Jews are not required to sacrifice to him. In fact, troops used to have to tuck away all insignia bearing the imperial image if entering Jerusalem, or even sometimes diplomatically enter the city by night.

Roman patience does have its limits. Any violence to Roman supply trains can lead to the people of the nearest village or town being evacuated, possibly sold into slavery, and the buildings flattened. A husband of a Jewish woman kidnapped by bandits/terrorists/religious guerrillas is required by rabbinic law to pay the ransom. If the same woman is unfortunate enough to fall into the hands of the Roman authorities, the husband is not so required. The bandits will respect the woman's chastity – the Romans very probably will not.

Summary

Perhaps through possessing a long history and tradition of their own, the Jewish people seem unable to appreciate the benefits brought by their conquerors. Their religious dogmatism inspires resistance bordering on and occasionally crossing into terrorism, and their propensity for wholesale and fanatical revolt makes many Romans wonder if it was worth bringing these ungrateful people the benefits of their culture. It does not help that many Jews also devoutly wish the Romans had not bothered.

✝ ✝ ✝

Where the whore sits, there are peoples, and great crowds, and nations, and tongues. And the ten horns which you saw upon the beast, these shall hate the whore, and shall make her desolate and naked, and shall eat her flesh, and burn her with fire ... And the woman which you saw is that great city, which reigns over the kings of the earth.

JEWISH INVECTIVE AGAINST THE ROMANS, *BOOK OF REVELATION* 17.16FF

✝ ✝ ✝

Notes

1 Just because a town was safe yesterday does not mean it will be safe today.

2 It's hard to tell which Jews are friends or foes. It helps that the Jews have the same problem.

3 If you must kill a Jewish rioter, do so with full respect for his religious sensibilities.

4 Try to fight Jewish religious fanatics on the Sabbath. They still haven't completely figured out what to do about this.

Berbers – outsiders in boom times

Briefing

Those expecting Africa to be a sleepy backwater of the empire are in for a shock. The place is booming, with entire new cities springing up behind the *limes*; the half-defensive, half-administrative line that separates Rome from Barbary. An African legionary of these times needs to be as familiar with a chisel as with a *gladius*, as there are new roads and new forts springing up across the fertile coastal plains of Africa from the Pillars of Hercules across to Mauritania and Numidia.

Many of the local people have adapted to the new Roman lifestyle, and Numidians with names like Rogatus and Fortunatus are by no means uncommon. But you have just to look at the tombstone of one of these men, which states that he died *gladio percussus a barbaris* (struck by a barbarian sword), to know that some of the indigenous peoples are not taking Roman occupation quietly.

Mauretania and Numidia and the other nations of that region, whose savagery never allows a trustworthy peace.

VALERIUS MAXIMUS *ON ILLUSTRIOUS MEN* 7.2.6

Combat techniques

The last organized resistance to Roman rule was under Tacfarinas, who was defeated in AD 24, but the Berbers don't call themselves the 'free people' for nothing. Those tribesmen beyond the *limes* are a constant challenge to the expansion of Roman rule. The first thing a legionary needs to know when he arrives at his new posting is the nature and disposition of the native tribes. Are they Garamantes, Lotophagi, Maces or any of dozens of others who can be peaceful horse traders one day, and then, through some sudden convulsion of tribal politics, lightning raiders the next?

The Berbers are above all a highly mobile enemy. They are superb horsemen. In fact the Numidians ride their horses without saddles or bridles and still control them magnificently while having both hands free to do other things, such as hurl sharp objects at their enemies. The average Berber is also a nomad. This often causes friction when they arrive at an oasis that they have camped at regularly for time immemorial, and discover that there is now a thriving Roman settlement on the spot. The natural response is to remove the settlement, and this is where the legionaries come in.

The Berbers have learned that a well-flung *pilum* can stop a horse literally dead in its tracks, and have become experts at staying just outside maximum *pilum* range and throwing their own lighter weapons into the legionary ranks. Consequently, the African legionary has learned the hard way to become proficient with a sling. Slings, often despised elsewhere in the army as a weapon used by barbarian shepherd boys, are light, easy to carry, and have a never-ending supply of ammunition underfoot. They are hard to use in close formation, but when a squadron of irregular light cavalry are raining javelins upon you, it is a good idea to open ranks anyway.

Because the Berbers are such keen horsemen, the legionary and auxilia cavalry are particularly important, and nowhere in the empire do all arms of the military work in such speedy collaboration. Because the Berbers lack the equipment to scale fortified walls, many settlements have their own mini-keep, and a legionary who likes an indoor life might become a specialist in maintaining and using the artillery there. This artillery usually consists of catapults that fire small, orange-sized balls of stone. These easily outrange even the best Berber distance weapons, and can cause considerable consternation as they rip into a tightly grouped raiding party.

[The Roman general] Curio followed the enemy ... onto the open plains. He was surrounded by Numidian cavalry and lost his army and his life.

FRONTINUS *STRATEGEMS* 2.40

Summary

A new dimension of desert warfare may be opening up with the introduction of the camel from the Middle East to north Africa. *Dromedarii*, the camel cavalry, have shown promising results against Berber horsemen, but it is only a matter of time before the Berbers start using camels themselves. How this new form of transport – which will allow the Berbers to travel even deeper into the desert – will affect warfare in the region is still unknown. It is certain that for the present the peoples of north Africa will continue to present two faces to Roman visitors – a peaceful native culture with greater or lesser Roman overtones, and wild raiders blowing in like a hot wind from the desert, tearing away at Rome's ever-expanding influence.

Notes

1 Berber raids are closer than they may appear.
2 Berbers treat selling horses to Romans as a form of economic warfare.
3 Life in a desert outpost consists of long periods of boredom punctuated by short periods of sudden death.
4 Never go far outdoors without a sun-hat and a sling.

The Dacians – see the Carpathians and die

The Dacians have always been about – the Greeks of 500 BC knew them as the Getae, and as early as the 2nd century BC they took on the Roman legions (and lost). However, over the past 20 years or so, it has been the Dacians who have been the aggressors. Their raids into the farmlands of

*Sarmatian lancers with scale armour (*lorica squamata*) covering their arms, legs, bodies and horses. Just because they are generally missile-proof does not mean that Sarmatian cavalry are either slow or clumsy. They usually have their own bows for long-range fighting as well.*

Pannonia have grown into small-scale invasions, and several legions are now stationed along the Danube trying to contain them. VII Claudia, V Macedonica and I Italica are heartily tired of dealing with their incursions, and XXI Rapax even more so, since it was nearly taken apart in AD 92 by a horde of Sarmatian cavalry – the Sarmatians being a warrior nation to the east of Dacia, and currently working hand-in-glove with their Dacian neighbours.

Briefing

The last emperor with the time and resources to deal with the Dacians was Domitian in the late AD 80s. He had to do something because the most recent Dacian raid to date had killed the provincial governor and devastated huge tracts of farmland. The two legions which were sent to deal with the Dacians had mixed results. V Alaudae ('the Larks') are not around any more because most of the legion and their general went into Dacia on a punitive raid and never returned. IV Flavia Felix went in after them and managed to even things up by winning a major but hard-fought victory. Despite this, the Dacian threat is far from extinct.

There was always the danger of the Dacians and Germans invading Italy from opposite sides.

TACITUS *HISTORIES* 3.46

The Dacians were not a serious threat until recently, as civil war was practically their national sport and these internal conflicts kept them penned in their kingdom among the Carpathian mountains. Sadly the nation has been united under a dynamic and warlike leader called Decebalus. This man has been far-seeing enough to make alliances with other nations, such as the Sarmatians, and has chosen Rome as the major target for his aggression. Matters have now reached the point where something must be done, and the legions are mustering under the personal direction of Trajan to do it.

Combat techniques

The Dacians' Sarmatian allies are horsemen who wear close-fitting armour that covers most of their bodies and those of their horses as well. They favour a long lance for close combat, but also have bows and light horsemen for skirmishing. The heavy cavalry work best as shock troops taking on slightly disorganized infantry, and their attack may well be in collaboration with Dacian infantry, who are more than capable of doing the required disorganizing. Legionaries from other parts of the empire might have seen an armoured arm-guard which some Dacian fighters sport as an optional extra. This probably evolved in Pannonia and is very popular in these parts as additional defence against the *falx*, a kind of heavy-duty bill-hook which some Dacian warriors wield with both hands.

Fighting those using the *falx* takes a bit of extra practice, and the Dacians also mix a goodly number of more conventional swords and spears into their ranks. Apart from avoiding death from any of these weapons, those fighting Dacians only have to worry about the heavy clubs and battle axes favoured by a minority (though it should be noted that many warriors also carry bows as an additional option). In terms of defence, the Dacians favour flat, highly coloured oval shields. Scale armour is popular for personal protection, as is chain mail, some of which was stripped from the bodies of Roman auxiliaries who had no further use for it.

Summary

The fact that Trajan is gathering ten legions to take on the Dacians is a measure of the threat this people poses to the northeastern provinces and the hard-pressed men of the Moesian and Pannonian garrisons. Anyone signing on for this campaign faces hard fighting and the expectation of death or glory (and possibly both). Be aware also that on the other side of the Danube, under the distinctive Dacian dragon banners, tens of thousands of warriors are currently mustering with the same expectations.

Notes

1 There are an awful lot of Dacians.
2 They are ferocious fighters who are quite capable of dismantling a legion.
3 They are well-led, well-armed, well-supplied and highly motivated.
4 They have sophisticated armour and fortifications, and the Carpathian mountains (which they know intimately) are well-suited for defence.
5 There are very many of them.

The discerning observer will have noted that the first and last points appear the same, but this is because (1) is just counting the Dacians while (5) includes their Sarmatian allies.

Parthians – warriors on horseback

The enemy uncovered their armour, and were seen blazing in helmets and breastplates ... steel glittering keen and bright, and their horses wearing bronze and steel plates.

PLUTARCH *LIFE OF CRASSUS* 24

Briefing

With every Roman legion that goes east march the ghosts of 20,000 legionaries slaughtered by the Parthians at the battle of Carrhae in 53 BC. As well as losing tens of thousands of men, the Romans also lost their general, the consul Marcus Licinius Crassus (and his son), their eagles, and about 5,000 men who were taken prisoner and mostly never seen again. Since that battle, no one has ever taken the Parthians less than seriously. Apart from their military prowess, they seem to cast a malign spell over their enemies. Julius Caesar was assassinated on the verge of setting out to campaign against the Parthians. Mark Antony, who did attack Parthia, came back with his tail between his legs and his army severely mauled. Soon afterwards he was defeated in a civil war against his rival, the later emperor Augustus.

The Parthians have responded to Roman invasions by launching a few of their own, notably huge raids across Syria and Judaea which were only driven back after desperate fighting. In recent decades, there has been an uneasy peace along the banks of the river Euphrates, which serves as the front line between the oriental and western empires. However, the rumour mill in the imperial palace on Rome's Palatine Hill suggests that if all goes well in Dacia, Parthia is next on the emperor's list of military projects.

Parthia is a huge empire which has its capital, Ctesiphon, near ancient Babylon and a hinterland which sweeps back to the foothills of the Himalayas. This varied and generally rugged terrain produces a commensurate crop of varied and rugged warriors – something which always astonishes soldiers new to the region who believe the convenient myth of 'oriental decadence'.

✢ ✢ ✢

Then the enemy set to work. Their light cavalry rode round the Roman flanks firing arrows, while the mail-clad horsemen in front wielded their long spears, driving the Romans together into a narrow space, although some decided to to escape death by bowfire by rushing desperately out to attack the enemy. These accomplished little apart from a speedy death from substantial and lethal wounds. The Parthian thrusting spear which they use against horses is heavy with steel, and often has enough momentum to go right through two men at once.

PLUTARCH *LIFE OF CRASSUS* 27

✢ ✢ ✢

Combat techniques

As a general rule such innocence does not survive the first Parthian cavalry charge. The Parthian army is run on feudal lines, and its warrior aristocracy lead from the front. These noblemen are superb horsemen as they spend much of their lives in the saddle, often on Turkoman horses, a breed famous for its size and stamina.

Parthian horse archer. The famous 'Parthian shot', which allows the horseman to fire arrows while in full flight from attackers, means that the Parthians can literally get you both coming and going.

Cataphracts

The Parthians have a variety of cavalry found nowhere else among Rome's enemies. There are cataphracts – super-heavy cavalry, with the riders armoured from head to foot, and the horses likewise protected under a blanket of chain mail. These riders carry a *kontos* – which is basically a sword on the end of a ten-foot pole with which they skewer enemies before those unfortunates have even worked out how to wound their well-protected opponents. If ridden down by cataphracts – and they take a lot of stopping – keep an eye on the butt-end of the *kontos*. This has a sharp point of its own, so that the rider can finish someone on the ground by straightening his lance and bringing it downwards. The good news is that with proper generalship, even a massed charge of cataphracts can be stopped, as was demonstrated at the battle of Taurus in 39 BC. The bad news is that it took 11 legions to do it.

Apart from cataphracts, other Parthian heavy cavalry has lighter armour, and is consequently more mobile. The lance remains a favourite weapon, but even on horseback the average Parthian is also a formidable swordsman.

Horse archers

If the cataphracts and heavy cavalry can be frankly terrifying, horse archers are both annoying and lethal. The Parthians use a recurve composite bow. That is, a bow that bends the opposite way when not under tension from the bowstring. It is a composite because it is made of horn and fibre glued together, with the result that it outranges most Roman bows, even if the Roman archer is on foot. A capacious quiver hangs from the horse archer's saddle, carrying a large stock of arrows and often a spare bow.

The horse bowman has the legendary 'Parthian shot' in his repertoire, which means he can shoot over the tail of his horse even as he is running away. The usual Parthian technique is for hordes of these horse bowmen to plague an advancing enemy with swarms of arrows, and gradually wear them down to the point where they are vulnerable to a cavalry charge pressed home. (The bowman carries a sword in his quiver as well, for just this eventuality.) Those facing a Parthian force have the iniquitous choice of opening ranks, which makes them less of a target for horse bowmen, but

De Res Militari

Tiw, German god of war, likes his sacrifices (on Tiw's days) as do Woden and Frey.

✜

To avoid nasty draughts, some soldiers fighting in the north are rumoured to wear trousers under their tunics.

✜

The Romans use the term 'Pict' as an unspecific description of anyone living in northern Britain.

✜

Claudius, Vespasian, Septimius Severus and Constantine are among the past or future emperors who know Britain personally.

✜

The Dacian obliteration of V Alaudae finished off those units which survived surrender to Civilis in AD 70 and a subsequent massacre in a German ambush.

✜

In later times Dacia will become Romania, and the language will remain very close to Latin.

✜

Falx originally meant simply 'sickle'. The Dacians appear to have versions that can be used with one or two hands.

✜

Trajan will write a book on his Dacian campaign, though this will not survive for posterity.

✜

When the Romans adopt the cataphract, soldiers will refer to the all-encasing armour as *climbanarii* (ovens).

✜

Because of the superiority of the Parthian bow over the Roman bow, most Roman auxiliary units now use the Parthian version.

easy meat for a cataphract charge, or closing ranks to stand off the cataphracts, but getting slaughtered by the bowmen.

*Let each girl know herself: adopt a reliable posture for her body:
one position is not suitable for all ... You too, whose belly Lucina has
marked with childbirth's wrinkles, like the swift child of Parthia,
turn your mount around.*

OVID *THE ART OF LOVE* 3.18

Infantry

Finally, there is the Parthian levy infantry. These too are stubborn fighters, but are easily defeated if the legionaries can get among them. This is because like the horse cavalry, the main weapon of most levies is the bow. The trick for an attacking legion is to have enough men alive when they reach the enemy ranks to be able to do anything effective when they get there.

Notes

1 Parthian infantry bowmen are a tough proposition.
2 Fighting the infantry bowmen is preferable to fighting the horse bowmen.
3 Fighting the horse bowmen is preferable to fighting the cataphracts.
4 Don't wait for the Parthians to run out of arrows. They have camel trains to bring reloads.
5 In summer, try to keep cataphracts on the battlefield all day. If it's hot in your armour, imagine how they're feeling.

✠ VII ✠

Life in Camp

nulli milites ad bellum parati approbabuntur a praefecto scrutanti sed nulli ad praefectum scrutantem parati approbabuntur in bello *

✠ ✠ ✠

Domus dolce castra

Keeping the *Pax Romana* does not require the legions to be constantly busy. Generally it is enough for them simply to exist. This allows the Roman army to keep the peace with an elegant economy of effort. A strategically sited legion might be based at a point where it is holding down several potential enemies at once. Should the legion have to actually move against one of those enemies, there will be nothing to hold back the others, and the situation can become very messy. However, the Romans can guarantee that nothing will be left of the original troublemakers except blackened and broken bricks where the cities once stood, and lines of crow-covered crosses where the former citizens of those cities have been nailed up. Consequently, outbreaks of violence are rare. The citizens stay peacefully in their cities and the legions stay quietly in their camp.

Since a legionary can expect to call such a camp home for years or even decades, it is worth looking at it more carefully. The first thing to note is that permanent legionary bases are not fortresses. Defence is not a major consideration in either the construction or location of a camp. After all, there is a *legion* inside, and legions of the 1st century AD don't need protection from anything. Such walls as exist are to keep unauthorized persons out, and to ensure that legionaries who are supposed to be within stay there.

---

* No combat-ready soldiers will pass an inspection.
No inspection-ready soldiers will pass combat.

Although there are individual variations, if you know one legionary camp, you know them all. Here is a quick guide to the standard model, which every legionary knows intimately (not least through building one every day while marching through hostile territory):

- The camp covers some 55 acres (20–25 ha). Allow extra space for those (rare) camps which have more than one legion – e.g. Castra Vetera on the Rhine.
- The walls form a thick rectangle with rounded corners.
- There will be gateways on opposite sides of the longer part of the rectangle.
- A road – the Via Principalis – runs between these gateways.
- In the middle of the camp, the Via Principalis makes a T-junction with the other important road in a Roman camp, the Via Praetoria.
- The *principia*, the legion's headquarters, sits at the top of this T-junction.
- The main gate is the Porta Praetoria on one of the shorter sides of the rectangle.
- The Via Praetoria runs from the Porta Praetoria to the Via Principalis.
- At the back of the administrative complex a lesser road runs to the back gate on the other side.
- Road and gate are respectively the Via Decumanus and Decumanian Gate.

The *principia* is the heart of the camp, and at the heart of the *principia* is the *sacellum*, the shrine which holds the legion's eagle. Other parts of the *principia* have administrative offices, and underneath, there is generally a cellar holding the legion's treasury (and there are few more secure places on the planet for a legionary's pension fund to reside). The legate of the legion lives not in the *principia*, but in the *praetorium*, which is generally a luxurious villa situated nearby. The houses of the military tribunes and the camp prefect line the Via Principalis, while the barracks of the legionaries are in rows closer to the perimeter.

These legionary barracks are the true walls of the camp, for any attacker must fight his way through these to reach the other buildings of the camp – the workshops, stables, baths and hospitals which are situated around the centre. There are about 64 legionary barrack blocks, each of which sleeps about 80 men and their officers. Every legionary can expect to become

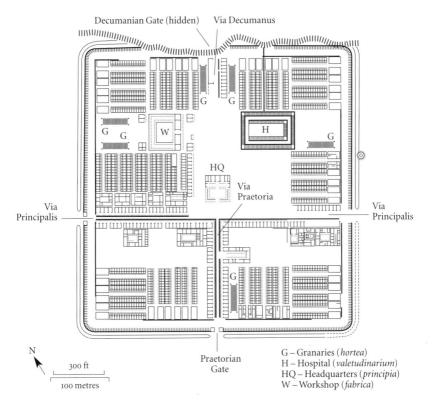

Decumanian Gate (hidden)   Via Decumanus

G   G

G   G   W   H

G

HQ
Via
Praetoria

Via
Principalis

Via
Principalis

G

N

300 ft

100 metres

Praetorian
Gate

G – Granaries (*hortea*)
H – Hospital (*valetudinarium*)
HQ – Headquarters (*principia*)
W – Workshop (*fabrica*)

Inchtuthil legionary base, Perthshire, under construction AD 83-87. Note the spaces which are available for either stables, workshops and medical facilities, or which may be left open as parade grounds. A distinguishing feature of Inchtuthil is that the terrain has made the placing of the Decumanian Gate problematic.

intimately acquainted with seven other men – these are his *contubernium*, the squad he shares a tent with in the field, and in the barrack blocks two little rooms of about 50 sq. ft. The barrack blocks are long buildings with a colonnaded veranda, and doors along the side opening into the rooms. Usually one of the small rooms is used for sleeping and the other as a living room and storage space. As accommodation in antiquity goes, this is not too bad. If you are lucky, your rooms might even have glazed windows.

ABOVE *Barracks. While life in the close-packed rows of legionary housing might seem insufferably cramped, the amount of elbow room is positively sumptuous compared to some of the tighter-packed parts of a major Roman city. Note the highly advanced and atypical crennelations on the walls and towers behind.*

OPPOSITE *In any army the latrines are the best place to take a break and catch up with the latest gossip, and the Roman army is no exception. Note the sponge on a stick which serves the same function as toilet paper in later ages. Take care to clean it thoroughly in the bucket before and after application.*

Duties

Just over 100 sq. ft may not sound a lot for eight men to live in, so it is just as well that they generally do not do so. First, the legions are generally under-strength, and secondly, some camps have a tolerant attitude to legionaries spending the occasional night outside the walls. Legionaries cannot marry, but many form long-term attachments with women from nearby towns. The authorities accept this, not least because many of the children from such liaisons go on to become legionaries themselves.

There is also the fact that for any Roman – not just legionaries – private space is something of an alien concept. Romans spend little time in their rooms apart from sleeping. Eating, bathing and meeting acquaintances is all done in public venues, and even going to the toilet is an opportunity to have a chat with friends, complain about the quality of last night's meal and catch up with the gossip of the day.

There may also be more elbow room in barracks than the architects planned for because much of the legion is not there. Because they are so useful to the peaceful conduct of affairs in a province, many legionaries are on detached duty. Among the diversions to look forward to while seconded from barracks are the following:

• Escorting visiting dignitaries about the province.
• Manning toll-booths and check-points on the roads.
• Sweating with chisel and mattock while building or repairing aforesaid roads.
• Guarding villages from bandits or barbarian raids.
• Protecting merchants with convoy duty along dangerous roads.

- Assisting building work in town.
- Being sent with a *vexillation* as a detached unit to help another legion on campaign.

These frequent absences mean that, for some legionaries, the camp is a base to which one returns at irregular intervals. Consider for example this record of T. Flavius Celer, of III Cyrenaica in the early AD 80s.

> Left for the granary at Neapolis (Feb 80).
> Returned.
> Went with the river guard (? 81).
> Returned.
> Duty with the corn commissioners (June 83).
> Returned.

The legion is a repository of trained men, from builders to farriers to clerks, and it is not unusual for any government officials in need of such men to look first to the legion to supply them. The legionary legate, who is himself a politician, is generally happy to do so as part of the exchange of favours which is the currency of Roman social life. Nor do the legionaries mind, as generally any break from the legion system and escape from routine is a change for the better. (Building work always excepted.)

For a specialist *immunis*, be he a medical orderly, groom or clerk, the legion is simply his place of work, where he turns up in the morning and works at his job until nightfall. The occasional intrusions of military life into this quiet routine are simply distractions that are compensated for by the security of the over-arching military superstructure that ensures a steady job, regular meals, medical care and a pension.

Troops load supplies onto a river barge. Those unfamiliar with life in the legions are often surprised by how much of a legionary's time is spent on manual labour such as carrying and digging and how little of his career is spent actually killing people.

The paperwork of a legion is managed with meticulous attention surpassing that of the corn commissioners or civil bookkeeping. Orders, military duties and finances are carefully entered every day. Even in peacetime the soldiers from all the centuries and contubernia *undertake their share of sentry duty, pickets and guard duty. To prevent too many duties falling unfairly on any man, and to prevent others getting off too lightly, the duties of each man are entered in the records, as also happens when he is granted leave, and for how long.*

VEGETIUS *MILITARY MATTERS* 2.19

About three times a month, everyone in the legion abandons the daily routine for an excursion called an *ambulatura*. The entire legion assembles in battle order, together with the cavalry. The legion proceeds about ten miles from camp, varying between regular military step and double time, while the cavalrymen practise escort duty, skirmishing and mock charges. After this pleasant walk is completed, the legion fights a brisk battle with an imaginary enemy, forming into battle line, charging (usually uphill, just for extra exercise) and rallying. After switching formations from square to line to wedge, the exercise is completed, and the legion returns to camp, with the officers chivvying the men to get back even faster than they came.

Daily routine

Wake, wash … and shave

The legionary's day starts early. Before cock-crow expect to be up, with your rooms tidy and your person properly groomed.

Breakfast

Begin the day with a light meal (probably of cold meat and cheese) prepared under the watchful eye of a military tribune. He has the job of making sure that the food given to the legionaries is of an adequate standard. (It is not unknown for the suppliers to use bribery to pass off sub-standard rations, and it is the tribune's job to prevent this.)

Parade

Fall in for the morning parade. This is one of the most important events of the day, since it is now that any major announcements are read out, such as letters from the governor or the emperor. The Prefect's orders for the day are given, and roll-call is taken. The watchword is supplied, and those who are detailed to leave the camp are told their assignments.

Daily duties

Once the major parade is over, fall out and head for a minor parade. This might be a special gathering, for instance a sick parade or disciplinary hearing, or a standard muster before the centurion to get the day's duties.

Sentry duty If it's your turn for sentry duty, presents yourself to the *optio* for inspection and prepare for a morning's mild boredom. There are two day watches – how interesting or otherwise these are depends on where the sentry duty will be. A goodly portion of time in camp is spent on guard duty. There are guards on each of the gates, guards on the ramparts, guards on the stores and the granary and in the sick bay. Other guards are on duty at the *principia*, and the *praetoria* (look especially smart for duty here!), while other guards accompany the prefect and the commander of the watch on his rounds.

Fatigues Fatigues are basically camp maintenance. This may consist of light duties such as sweeping or helping in the stores, or hard labour working the furnaces in the bath-house or cleaning the stables or latrines. Which of these duties one is allocated, and how often, depends on the centurion in charge. It is generally the case that the favour of the centurion can be purchased with a judicious payment, and lighter duties will be given in return. While some feel bitter about the unfairness and iniquity of this system, others accept that as long as the centurion is reasonable in his exactions, it gives a soldier a choice between having an easy life or a substantial pension. After all, someone has to do the dirty work, and in paying the centurion to avoid it, you are in effect paying one of your fellow soldiers to do it.

Drill and training This is something no one can escape. Legionaries are expected to be masters of their trade, and training does not stop after the recruit has mastered the basics of swordplay and javelin-hurling. After the morning parade, the centurion might send a unit off to training with a single word.

Campus means a day's work in the field, perhaps practising marching and fighting in formation, or conducting mock-fights with another unit. The unit might be taken further from the camp, to where there is space to practise putting up earthworks and thereafter holding the position against another unit who will try to force them from their newly constructed position. Since all legionaries are supposed to be able to swim, expect an occasional plunge into the nearest body of water at regular intervals.

Basilica means a day in the drill hall, and *ludus* means the amphitheatre. Depending on how the base is set up, either the amphitheatre or the drill hall will have the legionary doing exercises in armour. These might be yet more swordplay against that old friend the wooden post, running in circles at double time, jumping ditches in full armour, or simply general exercises such as seeing how quickly a soldier can get from tunic to full battle-gear in the event of a sudden alarm.

✣ ✣ ✣

Even in peacetime soldiers are off on manoeuvres, throwing up fortifications against non-existent enemies, exhausting themselves in pointless labour, so that when required they are fit and ready for whatever comes.

SENECA *LETTERS* 18.6

✣ ✣ ✣

Dinner

While most of the troops are on their duties, others are helping to prepare the late afternoon meal which is the legionary's main sustenance of the day. In some areas, one of the better and most exciting fatigue exercises of the day is to be assigned to a hunting party to bring fresh game – venison or boar – to the mess tables of one's fellow soldiers.

By and large legionaries in base are among the better-fed citizens of the empire, and depending on the nationality of the majority of his legionaries, the commander will take care to supply the men with items such as wine and the piquant (or reeking, depending on taste) garum fish sauce – beloved of Italians, but needing long-distance transport. Meat, cheese, bread and beer are all staples of the legionary diet. Pork is the most common type of meat, though what you get will depend on what is available locally.

✣ ✣ ✣

Please, my lord, give instructions on what you want us to do tomorrow. Are we all to return with the standard, or just half of us? My fellow soldiers have no beer. Please order some to be sent.

LETTER FROM THE CAVALRY DECURION MASCULUS AT VINDOLANDA

✣ ✣ ✣

Until bed-time

For those have avoided being on the night watch, the evening is, above all, for getting kit ready for yet another of the interminable inspections with which the officers love to plague the lower ranks. Since items such as mess kit are required to be in immaculate order, it is not a bad idea to have an 'inspection' mess kit, and another from which you actually eat. The evening is also a chance to catch up with any mail or parcels from home. Alternatively wander off to the baths, or – if the authorities permit – take your pleasure outside the camp.

I have sent you ... pairs of socks from Sattua, two pairs of sandals and two pairs of underpants ... Greet ... Elpis ... Tetricus and all your messmates with whom I pray that you live in the greatest good fortune.

LETTER TO AN ANONYMOUS SOLDIER *TAB. VINDOL.* II.346

Leisure

Most of the time an off-duty legionary can be found lounging around in the bath-house, which is not simply a place for getting clean, but also somewhere to get the kinks of the day's exertions massaged from one's muscles, have a game of dice and a gossip with friends, and enjoy a drink at rates which you can expect to be considerably cheaper than those in the taverns outside.

These taverns are in the village (*canabae*) which invariably springs up to meet the requirements of any army base, including the apparently insatiable need of soldiers to be scammed of their money in as insalubrious a location as possible. An off-duty soldier needs, in the words of one ancient writer, *amorant, potant, lavorant*, or washing, wine and a woman, though not necessarily in that order. Since soldiers are generally well paid and looking to blow off steam after the exertions of the day, considerable effort is made by the local entertainment industry to relieve the soldiers of their stress and the weight of their money bags.

This gift for the veterans and Roman citizens living in the canabae *of Legio V Macedonica was bestowed ... by Tuccius Aelianus ... and Marcus Ulpius Leontius.*

INSCRIPTION FROM LOWER MOESIA CIL 3.6166

Romantic liaisons with the female part of the civilian population vary in type, from physical encounters paid by the hour to mistresses (*focariae*) to women who are wives in all but name. Naturally, for no other reason than they are outside the camp, the diversions on offer in the village have a particular attraction to the soldiery. However, the authorities do their best to provide competition in the form of official entertainment. In fact one way of divining the political atmosphere back in Rome is to see how much money and effort the imperial authorities are prepared to spend entertaining the troops, though other entertainment may be provided by the legionary legate or governor on their own account.

Among the displays that might entertain a legion in camp are mimes and theatrical performances. (These are popular, particularly as the actresses are generally free with their favours. However, before he gets his hopes up, a legionary should remember that centurions tend to jump the queue.) Gladiatorial shows are well received, though the participants may be·slightly put off by performing in front of such a discriminating audience. Alternatively the legion might arrange its own entertainment in the form of inter-unit wrestling matches and military games.

Even though a legionary has a reasonable amount of off-duty time (so much so that in the east legionaries in permanent camps have been known to use their spare time and funds to conduct business ventures of their own), what most soldiers come to crave is the experience of being a temporary civilian once more. This requires more than a few hours out of camp in the evening, so the possibility of a week or two of annual leave is dangled before the soldiers to get them to perform to their utmost while in camp. Although a legionary who keeps his nose clean is entitled to his annual leave, the when and wherefore is at the whim of the authorities, who have

De Res Militari

A legion can expect to get through over 2,000 tonnes of grain in a year, so keeping the men fed is a formidable logistical exercise.

The watchword is changed daily. It is a basic security precaution consisting of a single phrase by which members of the camp can recognize each other in a hurry – during a barbarian night raid, for example.

✢

Retired soldiers often make their homes in *canabae*, so as to remain near to their former base.

✢

Although a *vexillation* is meant to consist of the best a legion has to offer, some commanders often suspect that the legionary centurions have sent everyone they are keen to be rid of for at least a while.

✢

One of the reasons for the Varian disaster of AD 9 (when the Germans destroyed three Roman legions) was that too many of the soldiers were on detached duties and were easily wiped out at the same time as the weakened main army.

to balance the soldier's need for a break with the overall manpower of the legion and the very real possibility that some soldiers may not return at all.

✢ ✢ ✢

If you love me, do your very best to write and tell me about your health.
If you care for me, send Sempronius with some linen clothing ... as soon as
the commander starts granting leave, I'll come to you at once.

LETTER FROM THE SOLDIER JULIUS APOLLINARIUS
TO HIS FATHER AD 107 *P. MICH PAPYRUS* 466

✢ ✢ ✢

VIII

On Campaign

nos contra robur exercitus Gallici pugnavimus: mille quidem contra unum
pugnavisse videbantur. fortissimus nihilominus erat Gallus ille *

✣ ✣ ✣

How to get ready

The Roman army does not go lightly to war, and tends to take the initiative in doing so (the tiresome Dacians always excepted). Therefore the legionary knows well in advance that a campaign is coming.

First, take the time to send letters to your loved ones, and say a tender farewell to your sweetheart or favourite village prostitute. You won't be leaving just yet, but you won't have a lot of spare time or energy in the near future either.

Second, and above all, eat like a bear before hibernation. A hearty appetite is a good idea for two reasons – you are entering a period where you will be burning food at an increased rate, and also the most secure way to take supplies on campaign is in the form of extra pounds of fat around the waist. Believe it or not, it is possible to be both fat and fit, and a legionary should aspire to be both before the army sets off.

Third, expect the legionary legate and officers to increase greatly the ferocity of the training routine. When the legions are about to start earning their keep, the commander generally moves the men out of the base and into

---

* We were against the cream of the Gallic army. The odds were a thousand to one.
But he was a very tough Gaul.

tents. A wise general knows that, especially with a legion that has been in permanent quarters for a while, it is a good idea to spend a week or two in the field for everything to shake down properly before any serious marching begins.

Sometimes this stage of preparation is severe enough to make the actual campaigning which follows seem light relief. The precedent for this dates back at least to the times when the Romans fought Hannibal in the late 3rd century BC.

He [Scipio Africanus] was not prepared to go to war until he had exercised his army with hard labour. He marched it all over the nearby plains, and made it build and demolish a new camp every day. From dawn to dusk, ditches had to be dug deep and then filled in, high walls built and then thrown down, and everything rigorously inspected ... the soldiers were split into groups each with a specialized task, some dug the ditches, others threw up the ramparts while others erected the tents. Performance was measured against the time allotted for these tasks.

APPIAN *IBERICA* 86

Everyone remembers the training manoeuvres of AD 57–58 when Corbulo kicked the somnolent Roman army of the east into becoming a lean, mean, Parthian-killing machine. So brutal were the training marches carried out in the wintry highlands of Armenia that some sentries froze to death at their posts. Ramparts had to be hacked out of ground frozen solid, and a forager once dropped his bundle of firewood and found that his frostbitten hands had come off with the wood.

Fourth, practise digging for victory. Battle drill will be a relatively rare event staged as a bit of relaxation between periods of intense digging. Roman generals are firmly convinced that the best way to win a war is with the *dolabra*, the legionary mattock. So when not digging trenches around the marching camp – ten feet deep please, and the centurion will be around later with a measuring stick to check – legionaries throw themselves into other exercises, such as:

- throwing up defensive ramparts.
- digging ditches to stop cavalry getting around the army's flanks.
- protective earthworks for siege engines.
- or perhaps a bit of engineering work on the roads and bridges that will get the army to where it wants to go.

(For example, the imperial engineer Apollodorus is even now at work on a bridge – over half a mile long – that will take the army across the Danube into Dacia – a bit of Roman engineering that will be around for a few millennia until the final remnants are blown up in the AD 1900s as a danger to shipping.)

Finally, the pep talk. When the period of intensive training has come to an end and serious campaigning is about to begin, a polite general should say so. This involves everyone being mustered in a special parade and being addressed by the commander. In his speech the general lays out the reasons for the campaign, why it is good for Rome, and how much booty will be available for everybody en route to a successful conclusion. This latter point is especially important if the general in question is preparing his troops for civil war in an attempt to take over the empire, as particularly lavish incentives will be required.

On the march

Campaign strategy

Roman military campaigns are essentially political, high-intensity warfare. That is, the Roman army at war does not try to seize militarily significant bits of geography, or chip away at the enemy's economic base with blockades and sanctions. Rather, the generals determine what the enemy will fight to defend – their capital city is always a good choice – and proceed towards it by the most direct route possible. At some point the enemy will put an army in the way and take its best shot at stopping the Roman juggernaut. The legions will chop aforesaid army into messy pieces, and the enemy will either surrender or its capital will be taken after a brief and terminally exciting siege. This bull-at-a-gate strategy has worked well for the past 500 years, and the emperor Trajan's approach to the Dacians and Parthians (or rather his approach to their respective capitals of Sarmizegethusa and Ctesiphon) will be no different.

The column of march

The legion is now formed into a column of march (see below) and heads off to war. Generally speaking, the column of march will change formation considerably once the legion is outside the Roman frontier, or if the legion is marching to counter an enemy incursion into its territory. The formation adopted will depend on the type of enemy against which the legion is marching. For example, when fighting an enemy strong in cavalry, the army might adopt a hollow square, with troops on the outside and the baggage in the centre. Obviously such a formation relies on the ground being open enough for the army to achieve it, but it is exactly this sort of open ground in which cavalry is most fearsome anyway.

In broken ground where speed is important, the army might be split into several columns with each making its way independently to the target. This approach assumes that the enemy is not strong enough to overwhelm one column before the others get to its assistance, and generally speaking the legionaries are less confident about this than their general.

However, the most common column of march is that described by the Jewish general Josephus in his book about the Jewish war. Josephus was actually in the Roman army which advanced on Jerusalem in AD 68, and as a military man himself, he knew what he was talking about. In Judaea the Roman army was advancing through hostile but relatively open terrain which could nevertheless contain some nasty surprises, such as the ambushing army which had chopped Legio XII to pieces at Beth Horon in AD 66.

Outriders and scouts The first part of the Roman army that an enemy scout will see is a reconnaissance force of auxiliaries and archers. The auxiliaries have the job of checking woodlands and other possible ambush points, and the archers have the job of covering their very rapid retreat if they should find anything.

Covering force This exploratory force has only to run a short distance before it reaches the substantial covering force of heavily armed infantry and cavalry following up behind. This unit is strong enough to stand off all but the largest ambush by itself, and failing this, hold out long enough for the rest of the army to arrive.

Pioneers Behind the sheltering force comes a small contingent of surveyors and workmen who will determine the site of the legion's camp for the night, and, once there, start marking out where tents are to be pitched and ditches dug.

Engineers and navvies Next, in advance of the army proper, is a contingent of harassed engineers who have the job of patching and making good any deficiencies in the road. These engineers are usually highly stressed since they are working against the clock to get things ready before the main force arrives.

Baggage train and siege engines These make up the most vulnerable part of the army, and the part the enemy will be keenest to attack. The baggage both contains loot and the supplies the Romans need, and destroying the siege train (and killing those who know how to operate its infernal engines) can seriously cripple an entire campaign.

The general Behind the siege train comes the general and all his cavalry and officers, so the engineers will be able to give their explanations in person to the commander-in-chief if there is any hold-up along the road. The general's position near the middle of the column allows him to proceed rapidly to investigate any problems or enemy activity during the march.

The legions From the legionary perspective, the good news is that with so much moving ahead the legions and auxilia can follow at a leisurely pace, usually ambling along six abreast, with the legions preceded by their eagle and trumpeters. Behind the legionaries come the mules carrying their personal baggage and tents.

Supernumaries Behind the legions come whatever allied tribes or supplementary forces the Romans are bringing along.

Rearguard To make sure that no one sneaks up from behind, there is another covering force of infantry and cavalry guarding the rear of the army.

On rough terrain where there is only a single track, a Roman army is stretched thin for a considerable distance. In extreme circumstances a large army might have ten miles between the advance scouts and the rearguard. Since an army on the march will hope to cover at least 20 miles in a day, this means that the front of the army is already halfway to its camp for the night before the rearguard has left the previous camp. However, such circumstances are rare. Generally speaking the bullock waggons and siege engines get the road, and the legionaries march on the ground alongside. This may sound rather arduous, but you will find that once a few thousand horses and the men of the preceding legion have gone over it, there is generally a very well-trodden path to follow. This is a pleasant experience when the ground is firm and dry, and very much otherwise if the ground is wet and boggy.

Marching camps

A Roman marching camp will seem very familiar. Not only does it resemble, almost exactly, last night's camp, it also resembles the permanent base the legionary has left behind. There's the same *porta principia,* leading to the same *principia* and *praetoria,* with the same people guarding it and the same people inside. Generally speaking, even the tents are pitched in relation to the old barrack blocks, and certainly in the same formation as they were last night. Thus, if Manlius of Titus Quinctius' century has the same size *caligae* as you and you want to borrow a pair, there's no need to ask around where the man's tent is – it's three rows up and two across, just as his quarters were when you compared shoe sizes in barracks, and where you went to share a beaker of wine after yesterday's march.

Of course, before the legionaries can settle into the cosy domesticity of their camp, they have to build it first. The new camp site has been carefully selected in advance for level ground, access to water and malleable soil. A defensible location is not a major priority, as the camp will anyway be highly secure once the legionaries have finished. In fact there are almost no records of a legionary camp being stormed as long as there has been a full legion inside it, though there are plenty of examples of people who tried and failed.

Where ladders were placed against the walls they [the legionaries] pushed them back with their shields and followed this up by throwing javelins. Those who had struggled on to the ramparts were despatched by stabbing with swords.

THE GERMANS ATTACK A ROMAN CAMP AT NIGHT,
TACITUS *HISTORIES* 4.29

When the legion arrives at the new site, work will already have begun. Each man in the unit knows what he is supposed to be doing, and some will peel off to find the mules with the tents, and others will head off for the approximate section of camp where they will be expected to contribute their section of wall and rampart. Generally the wall is made from digging up the turf and stacking it on to the rampart, though a bit of impromptu dry-stone walling might also be required, and the ditch walls made more solid with logs if the earth is particularly friable. Generally it takes about three hours to complete a camp, though it doesn't take the legionary that long to do his individual part of it.

With the same speed as they had advanced, the German cavalry tried to break into the camp at the Decumanian Gate. Because of the woods in the way on that side, they were seen only at the last moment before they reached the camp – in fact that the sutlers in their booths under the rampart did not even have time to retreat inside. Our men, not anticipating it, were stunned by the sudden assault, and the cohort on the outpost scarcely held off the first attack. The enemy spread themselves on the other sides to try to find a way in. Our men defended the gates with great difficulty; the fortification itself kept the attackers out elsewhere.

CAESAR *GALLIC WAR* 6.37

Building a home from home in hostile territory. One of the joys of lorica segmentata is that it is light and flexible enough for builders of a camp to work in full armour, and cleaning the armour once work has finished nicely takes one's mind off the troubles of the day. That seems to be the official line, anyway.

You will hear a lot of ranting about how much effort is wasted on building these camps, but generally speaking the army does everything for a reason, though sometimes this reason is somewhat unreasonable, or at least hard to comprehend. The logic is as follows:

1 Given the length of a column of march, there's going to be a lot of legionaries standing about while they wait for their fellow soldiers to arrive, so they might as well make themselves useful.
2 A legionary camp, advancing itself 100 miles a week into their territory, makes a powerful psychological impression on the enemy, not least because the Roman engineers will have spent a bit of time tidying and

straightening the road between the camps, even if the invasion is not a conquest. 'We are here', the camp says, 'and you can't do a thing about it'. To which the road adds 'and even if we are not thinking of staying, we have made a few alterations so we can come back more quickly next time'.

3 Then, of course, there is the effect on the legionaries themselves. Camp is a home from home. There may be a howling wilderness out there, populated with bloodthirsty savages. But the impromptu *taverna* that your messmates have clandestinely located near the stables on the Via Decumana is still there, and the guards on Tower XII still make a helpful clash of armour as they leap to attention to warn others down the line that the watch inspection is coming round. The latrines are now al fresco, but your favourite place near the corner is still available.

4 Ramparts and ditches not only keep the enemy out, they keep legionaries in. Desertion is always a problem in the army, and the prospect of going into battle and having lengths of sharp iron inserted into one's insides tends to induce wanderlust in the contemplatively minded.

Travel lodgings

Home is now a *papilio*, a tent, usually made of oiled leather (calfskin or goatskin are the usual choices), which sleeps eight. Eight is a tight fit, meaning that kit is generally piled up outside with the shields in their leather covers acting as a crude shelter over it. On entering a camp, it is often possible to see at a glance how damp the ground is. The muddier the surface, the lower and steeper-sided the tents become, since the soldiers fold the side walls inwards to make a 'mud-flap' that keeps them from sleeping with their heads on damp ground. Also, the lower the tent the smaller the volume within, and the better it can be heated by the warmth of eight bodies on a chilly spring or autumn campaign. In hot weather of course, the front flaps can be opened and angled to deflect a cooling breeze through the interior of the tent.

An important part of the tent's design is that the guy ropes do not go far from the main body of the tent, and every legionary soon learns exactly how far that distance is, and can negotiate his way home between the tent lines without tripping up. By now no one will be surprised to note that the

ABOVE The last thing many a barbarian ever sees. Legionary force in battle array as seen from the pointy end.

BELOW The *testudo* (tortoise) formation protects the legionary from missiles being thrown from all angles. Useful for assaulting cities or going for a stroll in downtown Jerusalem.

ABOVE A Roman vexillation (detached unit) in the field. Note the auxiliary at the rear. Auxiliaries are often locals, so he might be the only one who knows where the unit is going.

OPPOSITE The standard-bearers of the unit looking especially martial as they strut their stuff.

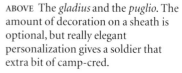

ABOVE The *gladius* and the *puglio*. The
amount of decoration on a sheath is
optional, but really elegant
personalization gives a soldier that
extra bit of camp-cred.

LEFT Side view of a Roman soldier
wearing *lorica squamata*. Note how the
baldric – the strap holding the sword –
is held under the belt to stop it
bouncing about. The sword is one of
the slightly longer old-fashioned ,
which is no surprise, as it is quite
possible for soldiers to have kit that has
been in the army for considerably
longer than they have.

ABOVE AND BELOW *Lorica segmentata* showing front and back views. The legionary in *lorica segmentata* may look glummest as he had to spend longest polishing his gear to get it to parade quality.

ABOVE RIGHT A legionary in *lorica squamata*.

RIGHT A legionary in parade gear. Note the decorative plumes and torques.

ABOVE Roman cavalrymen on patrol catch sight of a lonely Dacian scout in open country.

BELOW The shield should not be thought of as a purely defensive item, as this trainee discovers.

TOP AND ABOVE Artillerymen prepare a scorpion for action. The ropes of twisted hair and cattle sinew do the job better than any substitutes tried on reconstructions 2,000 years later.

LEFT A legionary demonstrates with a practice sword why an overhead stabbing action is impractical. Note the exposed armpits and kidneys.

ABOVE AND RIGHT And there's only another 140 miles to go this week … Roman legionaries in loose marching order. Despite being festooned with an abundance of kit, the legionaries can drop this, slap on a helmet and be ready for battle in 30 seconds.

tents of the centurions are larger and much better furnished that the average legionary tent.

Campaign rations

One major difference between a marching camp and permanent base is the lack of kitchen facilities. The logistical issue is something that has also occurred to those trying to stop the legions invading them. While the legion itself may be invincible, its supply lines are not, and no army operates at its best while its soldiers are starving.

✛ ✛ ✛

He fought by stamping on the enemy's stomach.

PLUTARCH *LUCULLUS* 11

Some ... said that they did not dread the enemy, but feared the narrowness of the roads and the vastness of the forests and that the supplies could not be brought up readily enough.

CAESAR *GALLIC WAR* 1.39

✛ ✛ ✛

It is in case an ambush on the supply trains is successful that the legionary carries up to a week's supply of food in his pack. This is apart from the dreaded hard tack which remains once the legionary has explored the possibilities offered by his boots and shield cover as alternative diet options.

In the field, the *contubernium* has to feed itself. Food comes from two sources:

The Commissariat Perhaps one of the most distinctive features of a Roman army in the field is how much effort has been made to ensure that food supplies are available for the army as it progresses.

• **Stockpiles** The general in charge will have ensured that before the first legionary sets a toe over the provincial border into enemy territory, huge stockpiles of grain and meat have been laid by to feed him all the way to his destination.

• **Food on the march** As the philosophical quartermaster will tell you, the true purpose of life is to keep meat fresh. Therefore he might lay on a herd of cattle to follow the legion, providing a supply of food that transports itself, stays fresh, and also provides a handy source of rawhide, sinew and glue.

• **Packed meals** The legion mainly supplies the men with grain and cured meat. The grain is ground in hand mills that are carried on the mule of the *contubernium*, and can be baked into crude cakes, or into a meal resembling thick porridge. A lazy troop, or one with a lot on its metaphorical plate, might simply boil the grain and eat that.

Forage parties Such a diet becomes monotonous after a very short time, and marching and digging for the greater part of each day definitely stimulates the appetite. Therefore the addition of fresh beef, pork or

Legionaries helping themselves to the grain from fields in hostile territory. During the Macedonian wars the legions looted so much grain that a Macedonian commando raid tried to set fire to the camp, reckoning it must be knee-deep in grain stalks and husks.

mutton, or an unexpected dollop of vegetable fare, is extremely welcome. This food comes from the land the army is passing through.

The average legionary will not see much of the enemy until he comes to a siege or a set-piece battle, since anything smaller than an opposing army does not stand a chance, and all the villagers along the line of march will have taken their women, children and herds as far from the advancing Romans as possible.

+ + +

Nothing distressed our troops so much as the scarcity of supplies.

TACITUS *HISTORIES* 4.35

+ + +

So this is where the auxiliaries earn their keep, as they work in forage parties, seeking out where the villagers have stashed their herds and bringing them back to camp to provide the soldiers with fresh meat. Other parties spread out from the line of march pillaging orchards and farmlands and coming back with fresh fruit and vegetables.

The spoils of war

This is one of the reasons why the summer and early autumn are called the 'campaigning season' – because the countryside holds enough food to keep an army in the field. The fact that this land has been farmed by people who need the crops and herds to keep themselves alive in the coming winter is not something that the average soldier thinks about much.

Nevertheless, the massive human and economic cost of having an army cross its hinterland is in itself a powerful incentive to Rome's neighbours to keep the peace. Having seen and inflicted such damage themselves, the legionaries and auxiliaries feel vindictively bitter toward the Dacians and Parthians who have brought similar misery down on the provincial heartlands of Moesia, Pannonia and Syria.

This part of the campaign is where the cavalry, both legionary and auxiliary, earn their keep. Both supply trains and forage parties are vulnerable to sudden attacks and ambush, as the native peoples unsurprisingly take a dim view of their countryside being devastated. (Although in some cases it has been known for the ruler of the lands being attacked to devastate the country himself at the start of the war, on the basis that the Romans are going to do it anyway, so he might as well stop them getting supplies.)

The cavalry are constantly busy protecting the supply convoys and preventing sudden raids from cutting down scattered forage parties, as well as carrying out general reconnaissance and manning the rearguard and advance parties. Generally, the cavalry have the consolation that when it comes to a siege there is little for horsemen to do apart from sit back and watch as the legionaries bang their heads against the opposition's stone walls, though when manpower is scarce, dismounted cavalrymen join the attack on the enemy ramparts.

De Res Militari

A legion on the march needs about 18,000 pounds of grain per day, 12,000 gallons of water, and 40,000 pounds of forage for horses, oxen and pack animals.

✛

Two teams of oxen working in shifts are needed to move 1,000 pounds of load 20 miles in a day.

✛

Because two *contubernia* in every century are on guard duty, a unit needing to travel light only needs to pack eight rather than ten tents.

✛

The main problem with ox transports is that the animals need to spend about six hours every day eating.

✛

To further discourage attackers the Romans dig small holes around the camp, cover the tops of the holes and plant sharp iron stakes (called lilies) at the bottom.

✛

Sometimes, just to really rub the point in, the Romans build their marching camp on top of a destroyed native village.

IX

How to Storm a City

munimentum intrantibus difficile est difficile etiam relinquentibus *

Eventually the legion will end up beneath the walls of the enemy's capital city, or some other substantial settlement along the way. Legionaries are generally ambivalent about sieges. On the one hand, storming a large, wealthy city wonderfully augments a legionary's pension fund. On the other hand, such are the risks involved that any pension fund at all might turn out to have been totally unnecessary. A siege is seldom a period of protracted idleness in which soldiers catch up with their correspondence and sharpen their dice-playing skills while waiting to see if the enemy starve before dysentery makes them give up the siege. (Even the Roman army – much more conscientious in such matters than most – has a deplorable habit of situating cesspits too close to wells.)

Rather, because of the up-and-at-'em attitude of most Roman commanders, you can expect sieges to be dangerous, uncomfortable, chancy affairs (and downright lethal when conducted by an incompetent commander), but they are generally over within a few weeks at most. Remember that Augustus managed to lose a grandson in a siege, and the emperor Vespasian's son Titus had an aide killed at his side. If those elevated personages are at risk, it is not hard to assess a common legionary's chances.

---

* If you make it too hard to get in, you can't get out.

Enemy general to the great Roman general, Marius: *If you are such a good general, why won't you come out and fight?*
Marius: *If you think you are any good, why don't you try to make me?*

PLUTARCH *LIFE OF MARIUS* 33

Taking a city is not like taking a barbarian encampment. Though barbarian encampments tend to put themselves on precarious and inaccessible bits of geography, taking them is generally a straightforward job for any decently sized Roman force.

    a Use the legion artillery to bash the palisade about a bit.
    b Lash together some scaling ladders.
    c Give an almighty roar and charge.
    d Fight a quick and relatively simple action.
    e Mop up and pillage.

The bad news is that there is almost nothing in these encampments to interest anyone who is not partial to pigs and ducks, while some barbarian women stash daggers in unlikely places – and are not afraid to use them.

Regrettably, assaulting a city is rarely so simple. Dacian, Persian and Greek cities (*inter alios*) have serious fortifications, and in Judaea the defenders provide fanatical resistance as a non-optional extra. These people know all about siege warfare – the Assyrians taught the Phoenicians who taught the Greeks and Jews who taught the Parthians (who were pretty good to start with). In these circumstances, nothing is more depressing than a commander who declaims 'we must take that wall at all costs'. The legionaries know who will be paying those 'costs'.

Preliminaries

Negotiate and intimidate

Generals have a selfish liking for taking cities intact, as these start contributing to the Roman revenue stream immediately, without the need for rebuilding (and repopulating) first. Any fine or ransom the city pays goes directly to the commander and the treasury, so the legionaries get nothing but healthy exercise from having marched to the city in the first place. It is important that, while negotiations are going on, the people of the city see the alternatives to surrender taking shape before their very eyes. So while the general talks peace, his legion is busily and very visibly working on weapons of war.

Build and dig

The opening stages of a siege provide a break from the legionary's usual job, which is marching long distances while carrying heavy objects. Instead the soldiers now go short distances while carrying very heavy objects. In a siege bravery counts, but so do engineers and builders. At this point, an average legionary won't be wielding a sword but his *dolabra*, and instead of a shield, he will be lugging wicker baskets of earth and large lumps of timber.

The timber is used for siege towers (of which more later), assembling heavy artillery, and not just for fortifying the usual camp, but making a series of camps all around the city, and joining them with walls, ramparts and trenches. If the city is expecting reinforcements, there will be another line of trenches facing the other way to keep those reinforcements out. Siege-works go up at an amazing speed – several thousand skilled builders working in shifts (non-builders stand guard for the others) can throw up five miles of wall in less than a week.

Wall and counter-wall

A good commander on the other side might build a counter-wall, which runs at right angles to the wall the besiegers are building, which makes enclosing a city more difficult. Pompey did this when Caesar tried to fence him in during the Roman civil war of 49 BC. He made Caesar build around the extensions to the extensions of Pompey's fortifications until finally

Caesar's army was stretched so thin that Pompey could easily break out of the attempted trap.

If he is expecting a long siege, the commander will be keen to stop anyone leaving the city – the more mouths to feed, the sooner starvation will break the besieged. At Alesia, in Gaul (and be thankful that these days the Gauls and their sturdily built defences are on the Roman side), the defenders drove out all but the able-bodied from the town. Caesar had already surrounded Alesia, and refused to let the women, children and elderly pass his lines. Eventually these unfortunates perished of exposure between the hostile armies. Sieges are a grim business.

Not only are the surrounding walls effective at stopping people getting out, they stop food getting in. In fact, the legionaries might even be set to diverting a river from its usual course so that it no longer supplies the town.

Stubbornness and surrender

Very often, just the sight of these preparations causes a quick surrender. With some generals the option of surrender is open to citizens of the besieged city until the first battering ram touches the walls – after that it is a fight to the death (their death, that is). Those who surrender quickly get mercy. A long, gallant defence can mean that the defenders get massacred. Along with their parents and wives. And their children. And their dogs, and their chickens. When, after a long, bitter siege, Sulla took Athens in the 80s BC, the blood ran so thickly down the gutters that it flowed in a small stream out of the city gates.

Roman arrogance and stubbornness has immense psychological value. In AD 73 the legions stormed the 'invincible' fortress of Masada in Judaea when the enemy could more easily be starved out – just to show the rest of the world that they could. A city garrison once boasted that they had food for ten years, but they still surrendered when the Roman besieger casually commented that he would inform the Senate to expect the city's destruction in eleven.

A reconstruction of Julius Caesar's siege lines at Alesia. Alesia was an example of a double circumvallation, where one set of lines kept the besieged Gauls in, and the outer circumvallation kept the Gallic reinforcements out. At times the soldiers manning the ramparts were fighting almost back-to-back as the Gauls launched simultaneous attacks from inside and out.

Negotiations might include the city's gods if the Roman priests decide on a rite of *evocatio*. By this the gods are invited to leave a doomed city and take up residence in Rome. Not all city gods get such an offer. The Romans may already worship the deity in question and so hope for divine neutrality, or the rites of the god may be too debauched (as with some Syrian religions) or too bloodthirsty (Germans). Bringing a new god to Rome is decided at the highest level, and only the Romans find nothing unusual in giving gods what amounts to a job interview.

Opening shots
Artillery

Types If psychological warfare fails, the artillery goes into action. Every legion has a selection of *ballistae* and catapults. Some, like the scorpion, are basically over-powered bows, while others are designed to throw rocks varying in size from a plum to a melon or even larger. There are two types of artillery – counterweights and torsion. Counterweights, as the name implies, require a heavy weight on one end of a beam to crash to earth so that the lighter end flies up and propels its load into the sky. Torsion weapons use the two most elastic substances known to the world – animal sinew and women's hair. These are braided together to make huge springs which add extra tension to the bow. Depending on design, these bows can either fire arrows (singly or by the dozen) or stones. Ever since they arrived at the scene, the artillerymen will have been preparing their munitions, and round stones, carefully sized and graded by weight, sit in piles between the ranked catapults.

Purposes Siege artillery has the general objective of demoralizing the defenders, and the specific purpose of clearing the enemy from the walls prior to an attack. Heavy artillery might concentrate on smashing away the battlements, so the enemy stand exposed on a bare wall. Lighter artillery is anti-personnel, and causes considerable shock and awe among those experiencing it for the first time. (And given what happens after a successful assault, there is generally no second time.) Josephus, the Jewish defender of Jotapa, records how a well-fired missile took a man's head off at the shoulders and propelled it clear across town. Eventually the force of the Roman bombardment made it too unsafe to venture on to the walls of Jotapa at all.

- -

OPPOSITE *Slingers eye potential targets. Though slingers prefer to use their well-balanced and lethal pellets, they can make do with any suitably shaped piece of rubble. And in a siege there is usually a lot of rubble on hand. Lead pellets often carry little messages to depress their victims further once the pellet has been dug out of their flesh. The example on the far right wants something bad to happen in a bad way.*

Counter-measures – the sally For artillery to work well, it has to be less than 200 yards away from the walls it is attacking. What artillerymen fear most is the sally. At some point the defenders may be goaded beyond endurance, and will then very probably swarm out of the gates armed with pots full of blazing pitch and a literally burning desire to get at their tormentors. Attacks can happen very suddenly, so it takes only a small lapse of vigilance by the besiegers before highly tuned machinery is abruptly converted into bonfire fuel.

Counter-measures – the slingshot Of course the defenders try hitting back from behind the walls as well. Slingers, rather vulnerable on the battlefield, come into their own in a siege. Their egg-shaped lead pellets do considerable damage even to an armoured man, and if they strike flesh, this closes over the pellet making removal a horrible business. The slingers know this, and their slingshots sometimes carry obscene messages as to which part of

Auxiliaries burn down a Dacian town. This form of urban clearance might be revenge for a guerrilla attack, or simply a way of encouraging the locals to move off their highly defensible hilltop to more unsafe but salubrious quarters in the valley where they will be protected by the Pax Romana.

their target's anatomy the shots are intended to end up within. On one occasion a pair of traitorous slingers within a city worked out that the best way to pass messages to the besieging Romans was to write the information on slingshot pellets, and fire them off in full view of everyone. This is one of the very few instances on record of genuinely friendly fire.

Counter-measures – fire Unfriendly fire is often, well, fire. Fire arrows (arrows with rags of burning pitch tied just behind the arrowhead) are shot from the walls in an attempt to ignite any wooden siege equipment within range, and though aimed at machinery, such arrows can also ruin the day

of any humans they hit. The besiegers might retaliate by lobbing pots of burning oil-soaked rags over the walls in the hope of setting the town on fire. The defenders hoist large sails of wet cloth to catch fireballs as they fly over the walls, and the besiegers cover vulnerable siege engines with wet cow hides to prevent them from catching fire.

Tunnelling

Purpose Meanwhile, there may be an even nastier war going on underground. Being put on mining detail makes other aspects of siege warfare almost pleasant by comparison. The objective is to dig a tunnel under the enemy walls. Once they have got there, the miners dig the foundations of the walls away, and substitute these with timber props. Eventually the sappers set fire to the props holding up the wall, and withdraw while the main army advances above them. If all goes well, the wall – crowded with defenders – will collapse just before the assault party arrives and storms across the wreckage.

Counter-measures – anti-personnel If tunnelling goes badly, the enemy has discovered what is going on. One way they might have done this is by banging a carefully shaped copper shield against the ground just within the walls. A light, tinny note signals that the ground below is not as solid as it used to be. With the besiegers' underground location roughly known, a counter-mine is started. The attacking sappers work in their narrow, dark tunnel not just with the constant risk of cave-in and suffocation but also with the prospect of an underground confrontation with armed defenders. Some well-prepared defenders don't go into the tunnels themselves. They send (for example) an enraged bear and a couple of wasp's nests instead. Alternatively they will pump the sappers' tunnel full of thick oily smoke and suffocate them before they can escape.

Counter-measures – lunettes Even a successful undermining can be made pointless if the enemy have detected it and built a new wall just behind the section scheduled for collapse. Such walls are called lunettes. They are curved like a crescent moon, all the better to rain missiles onto the front and sides of the hopeful assault party as it storms over the debris of the original wall. This is one of those situations where the *testudo* formation comes in handy. Thanks to their rigorous training, legionaries can make a *testudo* firm enough for a chariot to drive over the roof. This helps against even quite heavy missiles, but not if the enemy have had the foresight to lay on boiling oil.

Attacking the walls with machines

Battering rams

Together with an attack on the walls, the general might also try to smash down the gates with a battering ram. Battering rams are clumsy, and have to be capable of withstanding some very heavy objects falling from a great height.

Counter-measures When defenders see a ram on the way, they will lower protective padding against the gate or endangered section of wall, and also try to snare the head of the battering ram with nooses. It is a suicidal legionary who will pop out from under the ram's defences to remove these obstacles.

✢ ✢ ✢

The battering ram is a vast beam of wood resembling a ship's mast. At the front is a massive lump of of iron so carved to the likeness of a ram's head, which is what gives it its name. This ram is held in the air by ropes slung under its middle, and it hangs on this fulcrum like the crossbar of a pair of scales. Strong beams are positioned crosswise on both sides to brace it. This ram is pulled backward by the combined force of a great number of men who then swing it powerfully forward. There is a tremendous noise as the iron on the front smashes into the walls with irresistible force.

JOSEPHUS *THE JEWISH WAR* 7.19

✢ ✢ ✢

Siege mounds

If ramming and undermining does not work, the general might try a siege mound. This is basically a large ramp built alongside the enemy wall (while the defenders rain arrows, large rocks and everything including the court-yard fountain on the unfortunates building the mound). An ideal siege mound is made of logs laid alternatively longways and sideways, with any spaces packed with earth. The logs prevent the earth from spreading, and the earth prevents the logs from being set on fire. (Wood is so essential to siege operations that Josephus reports that after the siege of Jerusalem there was not a tree left standing for 18 miles around.)

Counter-measures The counter-trick is to undermine the siege mound, and remove material from the bottom as fast as it is piled on the top. Or, if the mound is right against the wall, a window can be knocked in the wall and earth and logs removed through that. Or sometimes the underminers will wait for a naive general to put catapults or an assault party on top of the mound before they collapse the whole thing. A basic rule of siege warfare is that no trick is too dirty, and for every trick there is an (often nastier) counter-trick.

But the city had long since laid in provisions of everything that might be needed for war. No defences made of wooden hurdles could withstand the force of their massed artillery. They had iron-tipped bolts 12 feet long shot from huge siege engines, and these embedded themselves in the ground through four layers of hurdles. In the end the defences had to be covered with bundled wooden logs a foot thick, and under this shelter, those digging the ditch could pass along materials. At the front of these works was an armoured shed, which had everything possible covering it as protection against the enemy's bombardment of fire and stones ... frequent sallies were made in attempts to set fire to our siege mound and towers.

THE ROMANS BESIEGE THE GREEK CITY OF MASSALIA IN 49 BC.
CAESAR *THE CIVIL WAR* 2.2

Attacking the walls with legionaries

It does not matter how large the attacking army, at some point the odds come down to the first legionary over the walls versus the entire defending army. That legionary is automatically given an award (the *corona muralis*) – but unless his comrades are very quick, it is bestowed posthumously. Getting on to the walls is generally accomplished by one of two techniques.

Ladders

Every legionary is gloomily aware that a particularly stubborn enemy, or a particularly impatient general, is going to literally send them up the wall. It needs only a moment's thought to realize how dangerous it is to climb an assault ladder with defenders waiting murderously at the top, which is why most legionaries prefer not to think about it at all.

When attempting to swarm over the walls of an enemy city, two factors are important – basic trigonometry, and the 12:10 rule. The trigonometry is to work out how high the walls are (calculated from the length of the shadow of the walls – though if the builders have been thoughtful enough to make the wall from regularly shaped blocks, just counting the blocks works as well). Once the height of the walls has been determined, the 12:10 ratio is for calculating how long the ladders must be – 12 cubits for every ten the walls are high. This is important. The futility of a ladder that stops six feet short of its destination is obvious, but too long a ladder can be even worse. Ideally a ladder should stop just a foot or so from the top of the enemy wall. Any higher, and a quick shove on the ladder by a defender (who sometimes carries a long forked stick for this purpose) and a dozen or so legionaries crash to the ground with an almighty clang.

At the same time, full battle kit weighs a lot. If you try to get a ladder that is too long just the right distance from the top of the wall by placing it at more than ten degrees from the vertical, it is liable to snap in the middle once loaded down with legionaries. Clang again.

The front rank advanced to climb the ladders confidently enough. However, it was a dangerous escalade, not so much because the defenders were numerous but because the wall was high. When they saw the difficulties this caused their attackers, those on the wall became more confident. Because the ladders had to be so high, many broke under the weight of the men climbing them. Others were made uncomfortable and distracted by the height they had climbed, and it did not take much to knock them off. The defenders discovered the trick of dropping logs or similar from the battlements. These fell down the length of the ladder, sweeping it clean of all who were climbing it. Yet nothing slowed the furious intensity of the Roman assault.

THE ROMANS STORMING THE WALLS OF CARTHAGO NOVA
IN SPAIN 209 BC. POLYBIUS *HISTORIES* 10.13

✢ ✢ ✢

OPPOSITE *Going up the wall in Sarmizegethusa. As the Dacian war reaches its climax, this mixed force of legionaries and auxiliaries make an attempt to swarm over the defences of the enemy capital. Well aware of their fate if the Romans succeed, the enemy prepare to throw them back.*

Siege towers

Given these grim odds, it is fortunate that the attackers can often rely on support from a siege tower. These monsters – some are six storeys tall – are the equivalent of armoured apartment blocks which are wheeled up to the enemy walls. The tenants of the upper floors of the 'apartments' are massed ranks of artillery, bowmen and slingers whose job it is to make sure that there is no one living on the ramparts once the legionaries on the ground floor push the thing up to the walls and climb up the stairs.

Siege towers must be immune to jets of burning oil, flaming arrows and the odd catapult strike (the engineer Apollodorus suggests using pickled cow's intestines as the hoses for fire extinguishers carried inside the towers). Yet all these precautions can be undone if the cunning defenders divert the run-off of the city fountains to make a boggy morass in front of the walls, or arrange a bit of undermining on their own behalf so that the tower heartbreakingly topples over as one side sinks under the ground just yards from its destination.

A general can guard against all that, and yet be undone by overlooking something simple. In the 70s BC, the Pontic general Mithridates was besieging Cyzicus when one very windy night brought his unsecured towers and dreams of conquest crashing down to earth.

Summary of a siege

1 Spend days, or weeks, building things while the enemy throws sharp and heavy objects at you.

2 Fight off occasional sallies in which the enemy attempt to burn or demolish what has already been built.

3 On the signal to attack, advance into a hail of arrows, slingshot and boiling oil.

4 Climb a ladder to meet a large number of desperately homicidal individuals waiting at the top.

5 Fight back down various towers and staircases to ground level.

6 Deal with last-ditch defenders on a house-by-house basis while the ladies of the household throw bricks and tiles at your head (it was one such roof-tile that killed Pyrrhus of Epirus midway through his last Pyrrhic victory).

De Res Militari

To destroy the morale of the defenders of Praeneste in 82 BC, Sulla displayed the heads of enemy generals on poles around the siege lines.

✠

When Caesar's men were besieged by Pompey, they tried to assuage their hunger by making cakes out of grass.

✠

When the Romans were besieging Faleria at the end of the 5th century BC a treacherous schoolteacher handed all the sons of the town's nobility to the Romans as hostages. The appalled Romans immediately released them, and gave the teacher to the boys for punishment.

✠

The Pontic king Mithridates besieged Cyzicus in 74 BC, and his besiegers were in turn besieged by the Romans. Cut off from their supplies, some Pontic soldiers allegedly resorted to cannibalism.

✠

To prevent the enemy ducking in time, Roman siege engineers might colour their missiles to make them less visible.

✠

The Greek inventor Archimedes used many ingenious devices to torment the Romans during the siege of Syracuse, including rapid-fire crossbows and cantilevered hooks that sank their ships. In the end just the appearance of a rope end over the city's walls would induce panic among the legionaries.

✠

Rome's enemy Philip V of Macedon was so good at undermining walls that he once persuaded a city to surrender by digging up a pile of earth and informing the defenders that their walls had been undermined.

6A Note that by now it is quite likely that – by accident or design – the city is on fire as well, so you are fighting people with nothing to lose amid burning and collapsing buildings.

Such circumstances mean that by the time they have taken the city, the self-control of the soldiers is understandably frayed. Ghastly things happen during the sack of a city, but a wise general will let it go on for hours, or even days, before he calls his troops back to heel – not least because there is a good chance that no one will listen to him if he tries to do it sooner.

Some were cut down by the infantry in the crush to get out through the narrow passage of the gates. Some did get out of the gates, but were chopped to bits by the waiting cavalry. No one was deeply interested in looting. The men had been made furious by [the earlier massacre of Romans at] Cenabum, and by the hardships of the siege. Those worn out with years were not spared, or women or children. Of the entire population, which numbered about 40,000, hardly 800 reached safety.

THE ROMANS TAKE AVARICUM 52 BC. CAESAR *THE GALLIC WAR* 7.28

After that, the Romans go about the business of pillage as methodically as they do everything else. Any survivors of the post-assault frenzy are rounded up and generally sold off as slaves. The booty of the city is collected together for later distribution on an equitable basis. Depending on the circumstances, the legion may then spend a further week or so levelling the city's walls and devastating what bits of the country that the army's foragers have left intact. Then, slightly less numerous, but considerably richer, the army moves on.

They exterminate every form of life they encounter, sparing nothing, but do not start pillaging until they get the order. When the Romans have taken a city, as well as human corpses you will see dogs cut in half and dismembered parts of other animals.

POLYBIUS *HISTORIES* 10.15

✢ X ✢

Battle

*tela vocari amica minime possunt, nam necesse est quidquam in te iniectum
hostile esse* *

A guide in four stages

For every legionary on active service, this is what it comes down to. Eventually, after months or years of training, the moment has arrived to do what the legion does best – face the enemy in the open field, and chop them into meat cubes. These are among the decisive moments in a legionary's life, and not just because, if things go badly, they will be the last moments. Fighting in a major battle is something to tell your grandchildren, a chance to be immortalized in history. When the name of the battlefield is mentioned thereafter, the legionary will prick his ears up and remark: 'That battle? I remember it. I was there.'

Stage one – overtures to bloodshed
Scouting

Because scouting is taken seriously in the modern Roman army, the general will have a good idea of the enemy army's position while it is still 20 miles away or more. Further patrols will have gone out to scout the ground between the two armies to see if a suitable venue can be found for bringing the enemy to battle. The commander may well accompany the scouts to look over the ground and the opposition for himself. (In fact the Roman general Claudius Marcellus was killed during the war with Hannibal while on just such a scouting trip.)

---

* There is no such thing as friendly fire – anyone attacking you is hostile by definition.

Preparation

The general might also send patrols with the deliberate intention of provoking a minor clash to measure the temper of the foe. Once it is clear that the enemy has decided on battle, locations of possible enemy ambushes will be discussed, and also the possibility of springing a few nasty surprises on Rome's behalf. There will be a constant coming and going from the commander's tent of messengers, junior officers and centurions whose role may be important in the coming clash. The medical orderlies will be stocking up on bandages, and sharpening odd-looking tools, the function of which every legionary prays he will never discover.

Choosing the moment

Sometimes this state of tension can go on for days, as the two hostile armies camp within sight of each other. It may be that one or the other army will march out and form up in line of battle, and the other will remain in camp. Often these delays seem inexplicable to soldiers with nerves already stretched like bowstrings. Were the omens from the sacrifices bad? Does the ground too strongly favour one side or the other? Is one side (let it be ours, please) waiting for reinforcements to show up?

✛ ✛ ✛

Every day Caesar led his army out on to level ground and drew it up in formation to see if Pompey was willing to offer battle.

CAESAR *THE CIVIL WARS* 3.55

✛ ✛ ✛

As the soldiers muster every morning, all eyes are on the general's tent, the *praetoria*. If there is a red flag flying, the commander will offer battle that day, and the legionaries, armour buffed, swords sharpened and shields polished, file out of the gates to take their positions. If the enemy start mustering opposite, then take a deep breath, and try to hold down your breakfast. The waiting is over, and a lot of people will be dead before dinner.

Trajan gives the troops a pep talk. The emperor is wearing the distinctive red cloak of a Roman general about to give battle. His words are given close attention by the standard bearers who will be particularly important in maintaining the soldiers' formation and morale during the coming clash.

Battlefield oratory

While standing waiting in your ranks, listen carefully to the general's speech. If you can hear it, this is a bad sign. The general's speech is an important morale booster. Since he can be heard by approximately one legion at a time, the legion he dedicates most attention to before the battle is the one which is going to be most in need of high morale once the killing starts.

*And now Titus believed that the enthusiasm of soldiers in war is mainly
aroused by hope and by oratory. Exhortations and promises often blind
men to even extreme risk – indeed, sometimes to despise death itself. So he
got together the bravest part of his army, and tried to do what he could
with his men.*

JOSEPHUS *THE JEWISH WAR* 6.1

From the legionary's point of view, the commander should ideally be a
distant figure, visible on horseback over several rows of helmets, and his
speech a few indistinct phrases blown his way by chance gusts of wind.
Remember to cheer lustily though, once he has finished. Let the enemy
know you are in good heart and confident of the outcome.

*He adjusted his rhetoric to best inspire the courage of the different legions.
The men of Legio XIV he called the conquerors of Britain, Legio VI, he said,
had taken the lead in making Galba emperor. And now Legio II would prove
themselves worthy of the new standards and eagle they had received. Riding
further down the ranks, he appealed to the garrison ... There was a general
show of increasing enthusiasm.*

PTELLIUS CERIALIS ROUSES THE TROOPS FOR BATTLE AGAINST
THE GERMANS. TACITUS *HISTORIES* 5.16

Stage two – opening shots (literally)

It is not a legionary's job to try to make any sense of the battle in which he is
participating. But since what can be seen of friendly and enemy formations
will give a lot of information about the chances of surviving until
sundown, it is advisable to get some idea of the battle-lines. It is an excellent sign if the infantry auxilia are lined up to serve as the first wave of
attack. Roman generals prefer not to spend Roman lives, and if it looks as
though the job can be done only with the auxilia then the general will

attempt that first. Remember that the auxilia are lightly armed only in comparison to the legions. Against the average barbarian foe they are heavy infantry, formidable both in terms of weaponry and training.

Formation

If the army is drawn up in a defensive position in deep ranks, then some hard fighting lies ahead. Deep ranks mean that the general is expecting the cohorts to come under pressure both physically and in terms of morale. Compare, for example, two battles against the Britons. In the decisive battle against Boudicca – who had won every confrontation with the Romans until then – the legions stood defensively uphill in deep formations, and let the British charge break itself on their ranks. At Mons Graupius in Caledonia, with the army brimming with confidence, the Roman auxilia charged uphill and broke the enemy without the legionaries needing to do more than applaud the auxiliaries' technique.

Skirmishing

Because of the range of Rome's enemies and the variations caused by individual commanders and terrain, there is no such thing as a typical battle. Nevertheless, it is traditional to kick off the proceedings with an exchange of missile fire between the light troops, and some cavalry skirmishes on the wings. (Roman commanders like to keep a keen eye on the cavalry battle – at Rome's greatest ever defeat at Cannae in 216 BC, the Roman cavalry was driven from the field, after which the enemy horse wheeled and hit the Roman army from behind, encircling it completely.)

Bowfire

In these early stages, those who are later going to find themselves in the thick of things might get an early indication of this from arrows dropping out of the sky, fired by bowmen some 100 to 150 yards away. These bowmen are not trying to hit anyone in particular, and arrows are seldom fatal if you remember to keep your shield level with your throat, but these arrows can cause unpleasant wounds to exposed limbs. Keep your head bowed while under long-range arrow fire. A bowed head can make the difference between an arrow bouncing off a helmet top or wedging in your eye.

Sketch of legionaries taking on a group of barbarian tribesmen. How the legion is deployed depends on the enemy and the terrain, but a good general will try to capitalize on the fact that the legionaries' ability to fight shoulder-to-shoulder gives them a local advantage over barbarians who fight with a wider frontage per man.

Barbarians clumping into tribal and family groups

Sally party, led by centurion

Cavalry

If the action is against those inexperienced in fighting Romans, the enemy leader might decide to blow a cohort apart with a ferocious cavalry charge. The sight of several hundred half-crazed horses thundering down on one is a truly terrifying sight. Yet even as an inexperienced soldier is considering dropping everything and running for his life, the veteran legionary is praising Jupiter for delivering the enemy into his hand. Cavalry have no chance against well-disciplined infantry in close formation, because the horses simply will not charge home. If the soldiers stay calmly in their ranks, the horses will screech to a halt in front of them, and the drill instructor's assurance that a well-thrown *pilum* shower can stop a cavalry charge stone dead will prove to be literally true.

Cavalry working around
the enemy flank

Military tribunes
watching developments

Close formation
legionaries five-deep

Reserves on stand-by

Counter-measures

Nor will the well-prepared Roman commander sit passively under this
early peppering. Roman bowmen might drive back enemy horse archers
and slingers, and the wicked field artillery weapons called scorpions will be
in action. The long, vicious high-velocity bolts are aimed to lower the
enemy's morale by skewering anyone in particularly ornate armour to the
three people standing behind him. Viewing the results is guaranteed to do
the legionary's heart good, even if the same cannot be said for his stomach.

The 'blast of war'

The noise, particularly from the enemy lines, mounts to a steady crescendo. The barbarians like to blow horns. The Celtic *carnyx*, if heard on a battlefield at all these days, belongs to a Roman auxiliary unit, but the Dacians have something similar. The Parthians favour a kind of kettle drum that eventually throbs away like toothache, while the Germans go a cappella with their *baritus*, a harsh battle cry given extra bass by the warriors holding their shields in front of their faces as they shout. Add to this the screaming of individual warriors as they nerve themselves up for the charge, and in the case of peoples such as the Britons, the ululating of the tribe's women as they cheer their menfolk on. Through all this, the Romans like to keep grimly silent in the fond belief that this unnerves the enemy. There will be the occasional sharp order from a centurion, and hopefully a yell of pain from the same as he gets an arrow through his toe. (In keeping with the Roman tradition of leading from the front, some centurions stand right at the fore, and their casualty rates in battle are considerably higher than the average legionary's.)

There was in Caesar's army a volunteer named Crastinus, who the year before had been first centurion of the tenth legion, a man of pre-eminent bravery. When the signal [for the charge] was given, he said ... 'General, I will act in such a manner today that you will feel grateful to me, living or dead.' After uttering these words he charged on the right wing ... Crastinus, fighting most courageously, lost his life by the wound of a sword in the mouth.

CAESAR *THE CIVIL WARS* 3.91–99

Stage three – combat

There is no saying how long all these preliminaries will last, but sooner or later – and usually at the first possible opportunity – the general will give the signal, and the cohorts will move forward in the slow deliberate walk which precedes a charge into the massed ranks of the enemy.

Moving to attack

Quite often the trigger which initiates a charge is that the enemy are preparing to do the same, and unless he is fighting with very green troops, a Roman general prefers to hit an attacker with a counter-charge. All this will seem familiar to even the most inexperienced legionary, who has practised every move so often he can do it in his sleep (and has virtually done so sometimes after a night watch followed by a gruelling day's training). As the Jewish general Josephus remarked, 'Roman battles are just drills with extra blood'. Trot, slow, hoist *pilum* step-step – throw *hard*. No need to look for a particular target – if there are a lot of the enemy out there, you are bound to hit someone, and if there are not a lot, they are doomed anyway. Now ... wait for it. There's a long drawn-out hiss all down the line as several hundred swords come out of their scabbards, and then, chaaarge!

✢ ✢ ✢

Then there was a deafening cheer; the cavalry hurled themselves at the flanks, and the infantry charged the enemy front ranks. On the wings they met only a brief resistance. The front ranks in heavy armour were more of a problem, as the iron plates did not yield to pila *or swords; but our men ... hacked at their bodies and their armour as if they were battering a wall.*

TACITUS *ANNALS* 3.46

✢ ✢ ✢

The charge

This is when the legion breaks its silence, and gives a mighty roar as the ranks complete the final yards at a dead run. Because the legion has been advancing in an orderly manner until now, the charging Romans hit the enemy as a solid wall of steel. On the other hand, the opposition may be somewhat more scattered, due to having started their charge as a wild run with the fastest and stupidest well ahead. (Or the fastest and bravest, if you prefer. On a battlefield, the two are very similar.)

The nature of a legionary charge is such that the first enemies do not even get the benefit of sword play – they get a solid body-check by a legionary who has put his shoulder behind his shield as the two men collide at a dead run. All going well, this knocks the prospective hero off his feet to be finished off with a brisk downward stab by someone in the cohort's second rank as the line advances.

Swordplay

As the enemy formation thickens, it's time to drop into combat drill mode. Punch at the enemy's face with the shield boss, and, as he raises his guard, stab hard and upwards into the belly with the sword point. Remember, this works even with scale armour because of the angle of stab, and from the point of view of a vigorously thrust sword point, chain mail is a loosely arranged collection of holes. Twist and pull to extract the sword, letting the carefully sharpened edge enlarge the wound. Try not to trip on entrails as you step over your victim and move forward.

In the melee

Inevitably over time, the line gets a bit more ragged, but as a trained legionary, it's your job to keep an eye on the men to your left and right. Don't drop back so far you can't cover them – especially the man on your left who might need you to guard his unshielded side – and don't get so carried away with bloodlust that you advance beyond their protection. And remember that when fighting almost shoulder-to-shoulder with your comrades wild sword swings are hazardous to everyone around, not just the enemy. While in formation, keep it simple, keep it stabby. Only if you somehow end up surrounded by the enemy can you start slashing out in all directions like a berserker.

And whatever you do, keep a tight grip on your sword and shield. Not only can losing either lead to fatal embarrassment during the melee, but also to awkward questions from the centurion afterwards. No one wants the suspicion of having deliberately dropped his kit so as to get out of the battleline. So shaming can this be that there are recorded cases of people who, having lost a shield or sword, persuaded their friends to help them plunge back into the enemy ranks and retrieve the missing items.

He noticed that his sword had fallen from its scabbard, and fearing disgrace, plunged back amid the enemy. Though he took a number of wounds, he finally retrieved his sword and rejoined the others.

THE SON OF CATO THE CENSOR AT THE BATTLE OF PYDNA 168 BC.
FRONTINUS *STRATAGEMS* 4.5.17

Under pressure

The energy boost from being in the presence of sharp-edged imminent death will, for the first few minutes, make shield and sword seem magically light, and nothing inspires all-out commitment more than that first clash of arms. In such an atmosphere, anyone saving a bit of energy until later is likely to find that for him personally there is no 'later'. But as the fighting settles down to a hard slog, insofar as a legionary has time to think about anything at all, it may occur to him that spending hours of practice slashing away at a wooden post with an overweighted sword was a wonderful idea. Otherwise by now an already tired sword arm would have dropped off, possibly with help from a barbarian blade.

Relief

If after about five to ten minutes the enemy are still obdurate, this signals that there may be trouble ahead. Generally speaking, with a legion pushing the other way, the enemy should be giving ground by now. From the point of view of someone in the front ranks, it may be time to allow someone else to take the strain. A wounded or near-terminally exhausted legionary has an option denied to those fighting opposite him. By bringing his shield forward, and then turning his body behind the shield, he can step back to the right and allow someone from the second rank to move smoothly in from the left. More often, this is done if there is a lull in the combat, and both sides have fallen back a few paces. Those dropping out of the front ranks should now take the time to check how much of the blood splattered over their armour and legs is their own. In the heat of combat soldiers can take astonishingly severe wounds which they only notice once these have been pointed out by concerned bystanders.

✛ ✛ ✛

A cavalryman was carried from the battle with a severe wound. He was taken to the medical tent for treatment, but was told that his injury would eventually be fatal. Having discovered this, while the shock of his injury had not yet affected him, he rushed back to the field and died after performing feats of great valour.

DIO ON THE DACIAN WAR OF AD 105. CASSIUS DIO *HISTORY* 68.14.2

✛ ✛ ✛

Driving on

In such cases, it is time to stagger back through the ranks to where the medics are waiting behind the unit, or, if still generally intact, to take a look for the unit's standards. If these are missing, things are going terribly wrong. However, it is more probable that they will be moving steadily onward, carried forward by the irresistible strength of Roman arms. By and large, the enemy front rank has the warriors with the best training, armour and morale. Get through that hard shell, and chopping up the rear ranks is relatively straightforward.

Following up

Once the melee has ended, pursue and cut down the fleeing enemy by all means. But take a good look around first. Victory in the immediate vicinity tells nothing of the situation elsewhere. Before bounding about in broken formation you might like to listen to the trumpet calls, which are pointing out – for example – that a squadron of enemy cavalry is shaping up to hit you in the flank. Generally speaking, unless certain the enemy rout is happening right down the line, it's a good idea to rally, lean on your shield and pant a bit. There is usually a second line of infantry in reserve to follow up any breakthrough, so let them come streaming past to take up the burden of any remaining combat. Leave the lads on horseback to track down and carve up up the fleeing enemy – they do it so much better. Relax and enjoy the amazingly euphoric feeling of being alive with nothing but friendly shields all around, and listen to the sounds of shouting and screaming growing ever fainter and farther away as the cavalry thunder past to follow up the victory.

Stage four – aftermath

Gallic and German auxiliaries might come trotting back with enemy heads bouncing from their belts. So prized are enemy heads that occasionally a soldier can be seen fighting while holding a particularly collectable head with his teeth. Even among the legionaries, everyone, once they have got their breath back, looks for a few mementoes, such as ornate gold or silver brooches, a particularly fine belt, or even a money pouch or two. Bear in mind though, that looting a battlefield and the enemy's camp is meant to be a collective enterprise. Not only those left standing at the end of the day, but also those incapacitated by wounds are entitled to a share of the proceedings.

Auxiliary clearly intent on getting a head in the Roman army. While these gory mementoes might seem to have a short shelf-life, the Gauls, for example, have ways of preserving them, and at least one Roman general has finished his days with his skull as a Gallic drinking cup.

The medic's tent

Fortunately for the wounded, Roman battlefield medicine is impressively enlightened. After all, its practitioners have had 700 years of experience to draw upon. Nor will there necessarily be a huge queue requiring medical attention. Casualties in a successful battle can be surprisingly light, since most of the damage to an army happens once it has broken and men are picked off as they run away. On the other hand if the day has gone really badly, then the wounded are generally left to fend for themselves as the survivors try to get back intact to the safety of the camp. Injuries are generally on the right (unshielded) side, especially in the leg. A sword cut is generally treated by an auxiliary medic, called a *capsarius*, after his *capsa*, a leather pouch containing bandages and medicaments. This man will clean the wound, often using wine, vinegar or olive oil, then stitch it up and wrap a linen bandage around it. Medical tools are regularly sterilized and are cleaned after each use.

BELOW *Surgical instruments. Two categories of servicemen know what these are for – the* medicus *and his assistants on the one hand, and on the other the unfortunates who find themselves on the operating table after a battle.*

OPPOSITE *Patching up the wounded in a field station. The poetic ideal is* dulce et decorum est, pro patria mori *(it is sweet and honourable to die for one's country), but this should not be because of shoddy or insufficient medical attention.*

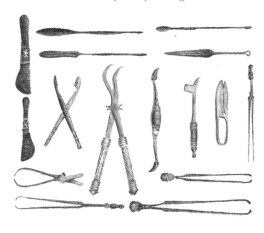

✢ ✢ ✢

If nothing else will stop the flow of blood, the veins must be seized and tied off on either side of the perforation, and if even this fails, then resort must be made to cauterizing the veins with a hot iron.

CELSUS *DE MEDICINA* 5.26FF

✢ ✢ ✢

Field surgery

Arrow wounds are referred to the *medicus*, a man with considerable medical training and centurion-level rank. He has special tools for extracting barbed arrows and is also capable of fishing severed tendons from out of the flesh and stapling them together. Doctors have a formidable array of forceps, retractors, scalpels and other equipment which allows them to

perform even 'heroic' surgery – operations in the bowel and chest cavity – with some hope of success. Poppy juice is a known opiate which is used to good effect, as is henbane seed (scopolamine). Despite these anaesthetics, such operations, together with amputations, are responsible for many of the more lurid screams coming from the medical quarters.

Hospital

Hospitals themselves are generally well-lit, clean and quiet, and the commander will almost certainly make a personal visit to check all is well, and to praise the wounded for their courage. Wounds are checked and dressings changed regularly, and facilities are provided for light exercise to aid with recovery. In short, the Roman army is one of the better places in which to be a wounded hero.

He [Hadrian] encouraged others by the example of his own soldierly spirit …
and would visit the sick soldiers in their quarters.

HISTORIA AUGUSTA *LIFE OF HADRIAN* 10

The reckoning

Once the dust of battle has settled, captured soldiers may be put to work tidying up the battlefield, unless the Roman commander wishes their dead to lie unburied as a dreadful warning to the enemy. The names of those Romans fallen in the battle are carefully inscribed into the legion's records, and their bodies await dispatch to the afterlife with solemn ceremony.

Soon after the battle, the commander will confer with his officers and parade the men. This is when the loot taken from the enemy – both from corpses and camp – is distributed, and when the general gives special recognition to those who have particularly distinguished themselves in the recent fracas.

De Res Militari

So effective is Roman military medicine that missile extraction techniques described by Roman doctors will still be used 1,600 years later, and Roman amputation techniques will still be seen in field hospitals in the trenches of the Somme.

✠

At the battle of Chaeronea, when Sulla's 10,000 legionaries took on at least 60,000 Pontic soldiers, Sulla claimed the Roman victory was won at the cost of 14 Romans being lost. (Though two of these were not dead and came back later.)

✠

At the battle of Pharsalus in 48 BC, Caesar lost 200 legionaries, but 30 centurions.

✠

Torques are designed to be worn around the neck, but on parade armour they are kept on shoulder straps.

✠

A *hasta pura* – a little commemorative spear – is given usually to centurions and above, though a common soldier might win one with a truly exceptional performance.

✠

At Pharsalus, Pompey's green troops did not counter-charge, so Caesar's veterans stopped in mid-charge, rallied, and then charged the rest of the way.

✠ ✠ ✠

After a battle … the general assembles the troops, and calls forward those he considers to have displayed particular bravery. He first praises the courageous deeds of each man and of anything else in their past record which deserves commendation.

POLYBIUS *HISTORIES* 3.39

✠ ✠ ✠

Formal awards may also be given at this point, especially if the battle has ended the campaign (this is often the case, unless the enemy has another large army available and is prepared to lose that too). The highest awards a soldier can win are crowns, but these – for example the Grass Crown for saving an army – are generally available only to senior officers. By and large, the average legionary will find his valour recognized by torques (necklaces), *armillae* (armbands) and *phalerae* (embossed discs worn on the uniform). Even these awards are available only to citizen soldiers, though auxiliaries might sometimes earn them for feats of suicidal bravery.

In this engagement Rufus Helvius, a common soldier, won the honour of saving a citizen's life, and was rewarded by Apronius with a neck-chain and a spear.

TACITUS *ANNALS* 3.21

Military decorations are well worth acquiring. Not only do they add special lustre to one's armour on special parades, but they confer status within the unit. This in turn means that the bearer is much less likely to draw latrine duty or a graveyard watch (between midnight and dawn) when standing guard. On the other hand, having a reputation for exceptional bravery means that you will be the first man that the centurion turns to when looking for volunteers for some particularly hazardous duty. As so often in army life, every benefit comes with its own drawbacks.

Aftermath

sunt milites veteres. sunt milites audaces. non sunt milites veteres atque audaces *

✣ ✣ ✣

Joyful and triumphant

Great victory or major triumph?

After a large-scale battle, the legionaries take careful stock of the enemy dead, and wait to see if the general will call a parade to commemorate the achievements of those who have won the victory. The soldiers look with tense expectation to see if enemy ambassadors will come to the camp to sue for peace. If the emperor is present with the army, the tension is even higher. There is a lot at stake here. Many of the legionaries have never seen Rome and speculation about that legendary city on the seven hills now reaches fever pitch. Everyone wants to see Rome, so they are watching developments closely and fervently hoping they'll go there as victorious soldiers in a Roman triumph.

Strictly speaking there are rigorous criteria that must be met before a triumph is allowed to take place. The most important of these are:

1 At least 5,000 enemy combatants must have perished in the battle.
2 The battle must have brought the campaign to an end.
3 The campaign must have enhanced the majesty of the Roman empire.

It is important for the emperor to be present with the army. First, these days no one but the emperor is allowed to celebrate a triumph, and while an emperor is entitled to celebrate a triumph won by his generals, he is much

---

* There are old soldiers, and there are bold soldiers. There are no old, bold soldiers.

more likely to petition the Senate to hold the event if he was present in person, or at least in the immediate vicinity. Secondly, he's the emperor. If the number of enemy dead was a mere 4,999, or the victory falls in some other way just below the exacting official requirements for a triumph, the emperor has ways of persuading the Senate to overlook these minor details.

To Italy!

For those in the ranks, the most exciting requirement of a triumph is that it requires not just the presence in Rome of the victorious commander, but also the presence of his army. Suddenly the legion is offered an alternative to chasing Dacian irregulars through the drizzle of a Moesian winter. And that alternative is the sun-washed shores of Italy and entry into Rome as a conquering hero. Regrettably, not everyone can go – the lines still need to be garrisoned, patrols have to be done and roads need building.

Therefore, among those whom the emperor will take back with him, priority is given to those nearing – or in many cases well overdue – the end of their service, and the wounded whose injuries entitle them to an honourable discharge.

Because the returning army contains so many soldiers finishing their terms of service, the march back to Rome has something of a festive air, though two-and-a-half decades of military habit prevent things getting out of hand. Excitement mounts as the army nears the city, and sees the great aqueducts of the water supply sweeping down from the Alban hills and across the plain of Latium.

How to celebrate a triumph

1 While Rome decks its temples with flowers and prepares for a huge party, the emperor calls a final assembly of the troops, and gives them the awards, commendations and share of the booty which they have earned during the campaign.

2 Sometimes, after a particularly spectacular victory, the emperor will have sent on ahead the booty he has captured for the state, and paintings and tableaux of scenes from the campaign. (The display of these through the city can go on for several days.)

3 Finally, the legions muster at the Temple of Bellona in the Campus
   Martius to proceed to the Porta Triumphalis – a gate used only for
   triumphal processions. In a triumph, the procedure is fixed – indeed it
   is reported to have been ancient even when father Romulus copied it off
   the Etruscans almost 1,000 years ago.

Now in the night time all the soldiers had already marched out in their
companies, and stood in their serried ranks, under their commanders,
and were by the gates ... And as soon as it was day, Vespasian and Titus came
out crowned with laurel, and clothed in garments of the ancient purple ...
[and went to where] the Senate, and the principal rulers, and those listed
in the equestrian order, were waiting for them.

JOSEPHUS *THE JEWISH WAR* 7.4

4 At the gate, the Senate meets the Triumphator (i.e. the victorious
   general). This man travels in the turret-like triumphal chariot, with his
   male offspring (if any) alongside him on horseback. The Triumphator
   wears the traditional purple robe of Jupiter, and has his face painted
   red, in emulation of that god's most ancient statue. To make sure that
   the distinction between emulating Jupiter and being Jupiter is clear, a
   slave stands holding a laurel wreath over the conqueror's head, and
   mutters quietly, 'Remember, you are only a man'.

Processional route of a Roman triumph

From the temple of Bellona to the Porta Triumphalis,
Through the city to the Circus Flamininus,
From there to the Circus Maximus,
On to the Roman Forum and the Sacred Way,
And finally up the Capitoline Hill,
Finishing at the the the Temple of Jupiter Optimus Maximus.

5 At this point expect a frustrating delay. Everyone, from the Senate to the trumpeters to even the enemy captives, get to go first, and the legionaries are left outside the gate waiting to take up the final station of the parade, and bring the event to a climax.

6 The soldiers march through the streets proudly holding their laurel-wreathed spears, and singing triumphal songs. Some of these songs will contain bawdy references to the commander-in-chief, who tolerates the not-so-subtle comments because, first, it's a very special day, and secondly no emperor, even as he triumphs, can afford to seriously annoy the army. The route is always the same, taking in some of the great open spaces of Rome, the better to display emperor and army to the adoring crowds.

7 Here, in Jupiter's temple at the very heart of Rome and her empire, sacrifices are made to thank the god for his benevolence to his people. These sacrifices include the Triumphator's golden crown, and several pure white oxen. As the Romans don't do human sacrifice, enemy leaders who have been captured and paraded may be strangled in the dungeons or the Forum, but as criminals and apart from the Triumphal ceremony.

The concluding pomp and ceremony was at the Temple of Jupiter ... And when they got there they stood still, as was the Romans' ancient custom to do, until somebody brought news that the enemy general was dead. This was Simon, the son of Gioras, who had been led among the captives, and tormented by those who drew him along by a rope about his head to a proper place in the Forum ... when he met his end, everyone sent up a great shout of joy.

JOSEPHUS *THE JEWISH WAR* 7.6

✢ ✢ ✢

8 After the ceremonies, the final prayers are said, and the legionaries are marched off to change into civvies for what will probably be at least a week-long party. This party may well include games at the Colosseum where some of the prisoners captured on the campaign will meet gory but spectacular deaths.

It is not just the triumphant legionaries who might attend the games that are almost certainly held at the Colosseum soon afterwards. It is highly probable that some of the prisoners taken during the campaign are there too, participating in the events in the arena. This packed amphitheatre is on a sestertius of Titus or Vespasian.

As any legionary will tell you, discharge after a triumph is the best possible way to bring a military career to an end.

Nunc dimittis

You can be dismissed from the army under one of four separate columns in the legion's record books.

1 *Misso causaria* is for those who have injuries that make them unfit for further military service. These injuries may be crippling, or simply minor inconveniences that make it impossible for a legionary to fulfil his duties properly. In either case, the patient is examined thoroughly before the doctors reluctantly announce that Rome will get no further return for its investment in feeding and training this particular about-to-be-ex-soldier. A *misso causaria* is an honourable discharge, and carries with it some pension rights related to length of service.

2 *Misso ignominosa* is not an honourable discharge. Quite the opposite. This discharge announces publicly to the world that the army considers the dischargee a bad lot and unfit for even military society. Certainly Roman society wants nothing to do with such a man. He is barred from living in Rome or ever taking up an appointment in the imperial service. Whatever crime caused this discharge probably also earned the perpetrator a whipping so severe that he will carry the scars for life as a further badge of shame.

3 *Misso honesta* is an honourable discharge. This is by far the best column to have one's discharge listed under. You have completed your service to the full satisfaction of your emperor and army, and are entitled to full pension benefits and other privileges that go with being an ex-soldier of Caesar.

4 *Mortuus est* is the alternative way to leave the army – by dying.

> *Old men, some disfigured by wounds, are serving their thirtieth or*
> *fortieth year ... there is no end to military service.*

PANNONIAN SOLDIERS AGITATE FOR DISCHARGE AD 14.
TACITUS *ANNALS* 1.17

Auxilaries get a special bronze tablet recording their departure from the army. Legionaries are citizens, and because the imperial government likes to believe that it keeps good records of its citizens in any case, no further documentation is needed. Records can always be checked – for instance in the massive records office on the Capitoline Hill. A man claiming to be a veteran soldier can have that verified by the relevant authorities on demand, and the record is harder to falsify than a bronze tablet. Nevertheless, some legionaries who are discharged *en bloc* might club together and erect a small memorial to the occasion.

A free man?

It's a big moment. Finally after a quarter of a century of regimented existence, with every hour of the day controlled by duty rosters and trumpet calls, the ex-legionary is a free man. He can decide when to get up, and what to have for breakfast. This sounds wonderful until the realization hits that freedom includes the necessity of arranging a bed to get up from, and sorting out something to eat for breakfast. After 25 years of having such details arranged for one, it's a bit of a shock to realize that they do not just happen automatically.

What happens next? Options:

1 Those finding themselves totally adrift in the trackless chaos of civilian life can take the drastic way out – they turn right around to the barracks and re-enroll. After all, a man who joined the eagles in his teens is good for a decade or two of further service.

2 Others might be taken up into a different type of institution, that of marriage. It is not unusual for a legionary to have a wife in all but name in the *vicus* outside the barracks, waiting with her toddlers for the

OPPOSITE *Trajan awards soldiers after a battle. One reason the general stays close to the front line during combat is so that he can take personal note of any feats of valour. Note prisoners in the background being hauled away to await their fate.*

discharged legionary to return and make an honest women of her. With his personal connections within the camp, and the lump sum of a pension equal to about 14 years of income, many an ex-legionary has started a profitable business supplying services to his former unit, be it the supplies of materials or creature comforts.

Many others have married into a business away from the barracks, acquiring a stake in a profitable concern and a wife from the offspring of their business partner. Those who might think of cheating a naive ex-soldier of his investment are generally deterred by the prospect of several hard-faced and unsympathetic ex-messmates of their victim coming round for a chat about where the money went.

3 Alternatively, there may be the option of starting afresh in a new land. If the army has just conquered a fresh tract of territory, what better way to hold it down than by settling discharged legionaries en masse in a new town? For Rome, it's a win-win situation – the legionaries get to stay with the kind of people and society to which they are accustomed, and in any emergency they can swap their civilian clothing for armour, and re-appear as a fully trained and operational corps. Naturally, the natives who have lost their land to the settlers will be somewhat resentful, but being conquered does that to people anyway, which is why the legionaries are needed in the first place. However, those settling into someone else's homeland should recognize that tact will be required before the dispossessed become integrated into the new world order and the economic boom that usually accompanies the romanization of a new territory.

When ex-auxiliaries attack

There's a reason why discharged auxiliaries are made Roman citizens on discharge, and it's not just to keep them loyal while they are serving. After completing his term of service, the former auxiliary knows the Roman army intimately, with all its strengths and weaknesses. This can make a former auxiliary a dangerous foe if he ever decides to return to his people and turn that knowledge against Rome. Rome came nearest to defeat in 90 BC when her allies rebelled, and Rome was matched against armies with identical weapons, armour, discipline and training. However, even individual auxiliaries can be dangerous if they go bad, as this gallery of infamy shows.

133 BC **Jugurtha** Jugurtha served with the general Scipio Aemilianus in Hispania, and distinguished himself at the siege of Numantia. He later went on to usurp the kingship of Numidia. After several years of war against Rome – in which he forced the surrender of the army of Aulus Albinus – he was eventually defeated by Gaius Marius.

73 BC **Spartacus** Reportedly a member of a Thracian unit of the Roman auxilia, Spartacus turned bandit on his discharge. Captured and sentenced to die in the arena, he broke out and gathered an army of escaped slaves and the dispossessed of Italy. He ravaged Italy from top to bottom and back again before finally being defeated by the later triumvir Licinius Crassus.

AD 9 **Arminius** This betrayal is still felt particularly keenly, as Arminius, a war leader of the German Cherusci tribe, was also a Roman of equestrian rank and an officer in the auxilia. He was trusted by Quinctilius Varus, and used that trust to arrange an ambush of three Roman legions which were totally wiped out in the Teutoburg forest. Arminius was later killed in faction fighting among his liberated peoples.

AD 17 **Tacfarinas** Formerly a trooper in the auxilia, Tacfarinas took to brigandage after his discharge, and became a constant thorn in the side of the Romans in Numidia. Army after army was sent against his highly mobile irregulars, but it took years before the Romans trapped and killed him at Auzia.

AD 69 **Gaius Julius Civilis** This man was a Roman citizen, but he induced an entire corps of Batavian auxiliaries to defect from Rome along with other units of the Gallic auxilia. These units besieged the demoralized legionaries at Castra Vetera on the Rhine and induced some of them to desert. The revolt was finally subdued by the Romans under Ptellius Cerialis, but Civilis fought well enough to bring about a negotiated settlement, after which he disappears from history.

Tombstone suggestions

Service in the Roman army is something to boast about all your life, but why stop there? Let posterity know who you were and what you and your comrades-in-arms achieved. The legionary burial club will have yielded enough money for a decent funeral and a basic tomb marker, but a little extra – perhaps supplied by your heirs as one of the conditions of the will – can leave a more impressive memorial. After all, you have spent 25 years as a component of the finest fighting machine the world has ever seen. You were one of the most feared and formidable people in the world – a legionary of Rome. You did it – so flaunt it!

RIGHT *Tombstone of Rufus Sita, Thracian cavalryman. Cavalrymen like the idea of passing eternity under a stone showing them crushing the enemy under the hooves of their steed, and tombstones like this are produced in large numbers.*

OPPOSITE *Marcus Julius Sabianus may have been a sailor with the Misenum fleet, but he and his fellow sailors were on occasion pressed into service as ad hoc auxiliaries, and as such Marcus is perfectly entitled to the shield and spear he displays on his tombstone.*

Ideally you want a stele (a mini-column) or at least a handsome free-standing stone. There is also, for those who prefer burial to cremation, the option of spending forever inside a stone coffin, a sarcophagus with four sides and a top allowing a full written and pictorial depiction of your career.

A cavalryman will surely yearn for a stone showing the glory days of youth. He can be depicted, cloak billowing, spear at the ready, crushing the enemy beneath the hooves of his steed for eternity.

Auxiliaries like to have themselves shown in full armour, but a Roman legionary might prefer to hint at his military past with just a few items of kit in the bas relief of his tombstone. However, the *armillae* and torques, or other decorations for exemplary service, make excellent borders to the stone.

Longinus Sdapeze, son of Matycus from Sardica [Sofia], double-pay soldier [duplicarius] from the first Thracian Cavalry, who served 15 years and died aged 40, is buried here. This was erected by his heirs under the terms of his will.

FUNERARY INSCRIPTION OF CAVALRYMAN *RIB* 201

It's also a good idea to describe smugly the easy transition to civilian life and give details of the family in whose bosom you have finally passed away after a long and successful alternative career.

The inscription can be fuller than it seems that space permits, because there are a number of abbreviations which make tombstone reading easy for those familiar with the conventions.

✛ ✛ ✛

L. DUCCIUS L. f. VOLT. RUFINUS VIEN SIGN. LEG. VIIII
AN. XXIIX H.S.E

[Lucius Duccius, son of Lucius from Vienne, of the voting tribe Voltinia,
standard bearer of the Ninth legion is buried here, died aged 28]

RIB 673

✛ ✛ ✛

Exemplum optimum

To the spirits of the departed	D.M.
Marcus Petronius, son of Lucius	M. PETRONIUS
From Vicentia, voting tribe Menenia	L. f. MEN. VIC.
Died age 38	ANN. XXXVIII
Was a standard bearer	SIGN. FUIT
Served 18 years	MILITAVIT ANN. XVIII
Legion XIV Gemina	LEG. XIIII
Is buried here	H.S.E

WROXETER *RIB* 294

1 You will probably want to start with the letters D.M. which stand for *dis manibus* – 'to the spirits of the departed'.
2 Then come the required details of name (*nomen*) and forename (*praenomen*) and mention of your voting tribe.
3 After this add a *cognomen* (nickname), unless your colleagues stuck you with something like 'squinty' or 'warty'.
4 Then give place of origin, rank and legion.

De Res Militari

Triumphs are not usually given for winning back lost territory, but an exception was made for Titus who won back Judaea.

The triumphal general's chariot is one pulled by four horses (a *quadringa*).

⁜

The arrogant intolerance of ex-legionaries settled around Colchester in Britain led to their entire city being wiped out during Boudicca's rebellion.

⁜

A general who has not won a triumph might be entitled to a lesser ceremony called an *ovatio*.

⁜

Tombstones do not usually list the cause of death.

⁜

Though the emperor alone is entitled to a triumph, the general who won it for him may be awarded triumphal decorations called *ornamenta*.

⁜

Serving soldiers sometimes prefer fellow legionaries rather than family as executors of their will, as these may be closer at hand when they die.

⁜

Many auxiliary tombstones have a mix of Roman and native styles in their carving.

5 Finally add your age and perhaps a mention of whether you paid for your tomb yourself or whether this was done by a grieving wife or heirs.

With the sculpture, make the bas relief as precise and accurate as you can, paying particular attention to items of armour and weaponry.

Future historians will be so grateful.

Finis

Milites! *Don't just stand there like a bunch of Vestal Virgins. You know what to do –
you've lived for it, trained for it, been paid for it. Now wait for my order ... and then
stick it to them! Trumpeter, sound the charge!* Unus, duo, tres ...

Roman numerals show the approximate areas of operation of each legion

— ·· — ·· — Boundary of the Roman Empire in AD 100 under the emperor Trajan

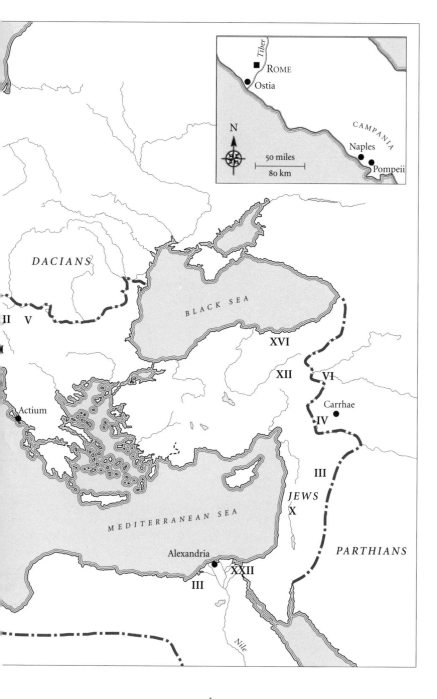

Tiber

ROME

Ostia

CAMPANIA

N

50 miles
80 km

Naples

Pompeii

DACIANS

BLACK SEA

II V

XVI

XII VI

Actium

Carrhae

IV

III

JEWS

X

MEDITERRANEAN SEA

Alexandria

PARTHIANS

XXII

III

Nile

Glossary

Actium the decisive naval battle of 31 BC which made Augustus and his successors sole masters of the Roman world

ala literally a 'wing' of cavalry

aquila the Roman legion's main standard. Carried by an *aquilifer*

armillae decorations for distinguished conduct

baritus Germanic battle cry

Batavians Germanic tribe divided into useful Roman auxiliaries and troublesome foes

buccellatum hard tack emergency rations for the desperate

caliga Roman military sandal

canabae facilities for entertaining legionaries outside camp

capsa pouch of kit carried by a battlefield medic

castigato a punishment beating

cataphract a heavily armoured cavalryman on a heavily armoured horse

centurio a century; an administrative unit of 80 men

cohort unit of auxiliaries, or one of the components of a legion

consul top political rank in Republican times. Consuls often commanded armies

contubernium eight men who share a tent or room in barracks

cornicularis trumpeter

Dacia approximately the area of modern Romania

decimation the killing of one in ten of a disgraced unit

dilectus an emergency levy of soldiers

dolabra entrenching tool

dromedarii camel cavalry

equestrian once a Roman cavalryman, now a social rank a step below senator

equites singulares Augusti basically mounted Praetorians

Euphrates the river that marks the Parthian frontier

exploratores cavalry reconnaissance unit

falx nasty Dacian weapon

Field of Mars the Campus Martius, where the Romans came to vote and practise military exercises

framea German battle spear

furca stick for carrying a legionary pack

fustuarium severe (sometimes fatal) punishment beating

gladius (Hispaniensis) legionary sword

Illyria in the area of modern Croatia

immunis soldier with special duties

legate the commander of a legion

lorica armour, usually *segmentata* (legionary), *hamata* (mail) or *squamata* (scale)

maniple obsolete fighting unit of 120 men

Marius, Gaius general who made far-reaching changes to the Roman army

miles gregarius common soldier

Military Tribune one of the senior officers in a legion. Commands one or two cohorts in battle

misso honesta honourable discharge

misso ignominosa discharge in disgrace

munerum indictio extra duties given as punishment

munifex a soldier with absolutely no rank or privileges

Numidia African state in the area of modern Lybia and Tunisia

Pannonia a Roman province between the Balkans and Romania

papilio small campaign tent. Sleeps eight, provided no-one has been eating beans

Parthia a powerful kingdom east of the Roman empire

patera all-purpose mess-tin and drinking bowl

pedites infantrymen

peregrinus a non-citizen passing through or resident on Roman territory

phalanx any solid block of ancient spearmen. A formation brought to its peak by the Macedonians

phalerae decorations for distinguished conduct

Pharsalus the battle which won the civil wars for Julius Caesar

Pict warlike inhabitant of Caledonia

pilum legionary spear

praetorium general's campaign tent

praefectus castrorum in charge of the day-to-day running of the camp

primus pilus senior centurion in a legion

principia legion headquarters

probatio test for suitability as a legionary

puglio dagger

Sarmatians a warrior people from the north of the Black Sea

scutum shield

sicarius fanatical Jewish freedom fighter

signifer standard bearer

spatha cavalry sword

tribunus laticlavus second-in-command of a legion

triumviral relating to the Triumvirs. These were unions of powerful politicians who attempted to unite the world under their rule, but ended up fighting with each other over the spoils

turma a cavalry troop

Vetera a large legionary camp on the Rhine

vexillationes small units assembled *ad hoc* for special purposes

viaticum travel money for new recruits

vitis centurion's vine-wood staff

voluntarii recruits who actually want to join the army

Acknowledgments

Writing this book has been made easier by the kind help given to me by enthusiasts of Roman military history, whether these be fellow historians or Roman army re-enactors and those who make their equipment. They have provided me with 'hands on' details that would have been impossible to come by otherwise. If this book gives a genuine feeling of how it was to march in armour carrying a heavy pack, those who have actually done it are the people to thank. Foremost amongst those who gently corrected my ignorance of matters military are Nigel Berry and Adrian Goldsworthy, the latter assisting me both in person and with his books such as *The Complete Roman Army*, *In the Name of Rome*, and *Roman Warfare*.

Further Reading

Roman warfare is something that Romans loved to write about, often from personal experience. Here are the top ten essential books for the would-be legionary.

Tacitus, *The Histories*, *The Annals*, *Germania* and *Agricola*. Though not a military man himself, Tacitus gives stirring accounts of battles, sometimes based on direct interviews with the participants.

Julius Caesar, *The Gallic War*, *The Civil War*. Written personally by one of the best generals in antiquity – what more could one ask for?

Josephus, *The Jewish War*. He not only led an army against the Romans but he lived to tell the tale. Another first-person account of Rome at war.

Sallust, *The War against Jugurtha*. Military history and politics mix in this account of a war in Africa by a soldier and statesman.

Polybius, *The Histories*. Look especially at his accounts of the later Macedonian Wars – he saw parts of these campaigns for himself.

Arrian, *Array against the Alans*. An eyewitness account of a Roman army on the move by one of the best military historians in antiquity.

Frontinus, *The Strategems*. A collection of military anecdotes by an ex-General who later went on to become Rome's aqueduct manager.

Vitruvius, *De Architectura*. Dry as dust for the most part, but turn to chapter X and read all about seiges and siege artillery.

Plutarch, *Roman Lives*. Though not a military man, Plutarch's biographies have details of battles and incidents which do not exist elsewhere.

Ammianus Marcellinus, *History*. The greatest military historian of the late empire tells of his campaigns against the Persians.

Sources of Illustrations

Index